Tante Johanne

Tante Johanne

Letters of a Danish Immigrant Family
1887-1910

A family heritage is a precious possession

Edited by
John W. Nielsen

John W. Nielsen

Lur Publications
Danish Immigrant Archive

Dana College, Blair, Nebraska

Published by Lur Publications, Dana College, Blair, Nebraska, 68008.

First edition.

Second Printing

ISBN 0-930697-01-4

Logo designed by Elizabeth Solevad Nielsen
Designed by Mercury Media, Ltd., 2066 Colfax St., Blair, NE 68008
Printed by MicroSmart Printing & Graphics, 1740 Washington St., Blair, NE 68008

Printed in the United States of America

Dedicated to the Memory
of
My Father and Mother-in-law,
Einar Solevad and Else Poulsen,
and
My Father, John Nielsen,
Immigrants from Denmark,
and
My Mother, Meta Wolter,
Daughter of German Immigrants

Contents

viii

ILLUSTRATIONS

Preface

Letters have bridged the Atlantic since the earliest days of Danish immigration, and they are documents of great historical interest because they express the thoughts and experiences of the immigrants in their own words. In these letters, as H. Arnold Barton put it, "for the first time in human history, (common people) began to speak directly to posterity."

Danish immigrant letters are unusually rich because Denmark had the first sound system of public education in Europe, so Danish immigrants were well prepared to express themselves. Many collections of Danish immigrant letters have been published, most of them in the Danish language, but no two collections are alike because every letter writer and every editor is different. The writers varied in their personalities, experiences, and abilities to put their feelings and observations into words. The editors have applied various principles, some using whole letters, others fragments, some arranging them chronologically, others topically or by writers, and some including photographs, maps, charts, and commentary to supplement the text.

This book is important because it represents the first fruits of the largest collection of family correspondence known to American immigration scholarship: the Hansen-Mengers collection of over 12,000 letters in the Danish Immigrant Archive-Dana College. Other publications from this collection will follow in the years to come. Numerous family photographs bring us face to face with the writers in this volume, and the character of each comes through in the letters: Johanne Nielsen's emotional piety and longing for her native Denmark, the lively energy of her daughters, the narrative skill of the brothers Mengers, and the critical attitude towards America of their brother Niels, back in Denmark. The editor deftly introduces every letter, reveals changes in time by following a chronological order, and sketches rich context ranging from the daily activities of pioneer farm women to railroads, rural schools, prices, immigrant publications, the Inner Mission, the Panic of 1893, and the Spanish-American War.

Let the Danish pioneers speak to you as you savor their letters from a century ago.

J. R. Christianson
Luther College
Decorah, Iowa

Editor's Notes
and Acknowledgments

From the moment I first sampled a few of the 12,000 letters in the then recently acquired Hansen-Mengers Collection, the idea of a book such as this seized me. Its realization, however, had to be postponed. The immediate task was the cataloging of the collection. Next letters that offered a unity of theme had to be identified. Only then could the painstaking process of translating and editing begin. At that point, however, an initial but crucial decision had to be made. Who was the intended audience? Two obvious and legitimate candidates immediately presented themselves - the general public and the scholarly community. Because of the collection's deep roots in the fabric of Danish immigrant society and in the Danish Lutheran Church, I have made the general reader of Danish descent the principal intended audience. I must confess, however, that I hope the contents of the book also will be of interest to immigrant scholars. Perhaps this dual thrust is a mistake. Only time will tell.

Many individuals have contributed to the completion of the above tasks and to the preparation of this book. I am deeply indebted in various ways to each of them. Their names appear on the last page of this book for they are the individuals who enable the Dana College Library and its Danish Immigrant Archive to be the fine centers of learning and research that they are. So to each of them I extend my thanks.

There are, however, certain individuals that I must cite for special assistance. Sara Hansen-Walter has been indispensable in providing family information and pictures of Tante Johanne's family of which she is a member; Susan Legore has helped to locate information on Algona and Kossuth County, Iowa; and Sharon Jensen has provided essential general information. She and her husband, Tim Jensen, assumed the tedious task of doing the final proof-reading. While performing this task, they made several valuable suggestions that have been incorporated into the text. Each of these individuals has my sincere thanks.

All the letters with the exception of those written by Carol, Julia, and Gertrude Nielsen had to be translated from Danish. This indispensable task was done by a number of individuals, but because more than one worked on any given letter over the years, it is impossible to attribute any letter to a single person. My deepest gratitude, however, goes to each of the following, Birgitte Andreasen, Ninna Engskow, Johanne Haas, Kirstin Kristensen, Merete Larsen, Inga Larsen, John Mark Nielsen, and Dorte Staermose. Although they did the work, I must assume full responsibility for the final form of the printed texts.

The painstaking process of entering the texts of the letters was done by Dolores Johnson and Erik Nielsen who have earned my gratitude not only for the work they did but for patiently deciphering my scribbled notes and corrections.

I hope Ruth Rasmussen, Dana librarian, knows how appreciative I have been of her unstinting support, her generous offer of personnel, materials, and facilities, and perhaps above all for her sustained enthusiasm for this project. Similarly, I have experienced nothing but encouragement and support from Dr. Myrvin Christopherson and from Dr. Paul Formo, the President and the Dean of Academic Affairs of Dana College. This, of course, was most encouraging.

Finally, three members of my own family performed invaluable service in the completion of this book, rescuing me more often than I like to recall. They are my two eldest sons and my wife. John Mark, a member of the English department and a student of Danish immigration, provided indispensable criticism, assistance, and insight as well as taking the pictures of Tante Johanne's grave and of the Des Moines River. Thomas, a member of the library staff and a former editor, carried the brunt of publishing preparations and arrangements that brought the book to completion, as well as making valuable textual suggestions while the work was in process. Elizabeth not only designed the logo for Lur Publications but provided daily encouragement, understanding and assistance as I experienced the inevitable ups and downs that accompany the editing process. Because of my special gratitude to them, I dedicate this book to our parents and to the grandparents of our five children.

In conclusion it is necessary to indicate that in translating and editing these letters the following procedures have been observed:

1. Grammar, punctuation, and capitalization have been altered when necessary for clarity.
2. Misspellings in the English letters have been changed only when the original might lead to misunderstandings.
3. Paragraph structure has been added.
4 . Names and the spellings of names have been retained even when a writer is inconsistent though the more common name has been provided in parentheses.
5. Openings and closings have been separated from the body of the letter where they often appear and are standardized with place and state or country followed by the date which is given as month, day and year.
6. The use of numerals in the text has been retained when used by a writer.
7. Illegible passages are noted in parentheses and uncertain transcriptions are followed by question marks.
8. In the body of the book texts of letters are set in regular type; editorial comments, in italics.
9. At the end of each letter the Danish Immigrant Archive - Dana College collection number appears (HAN 988) followed by numbers indicating the box, packet, and individual letter and the language in which the letter was written.

John W. Nielsen
September 9, 1996

Tante Johanne
Johanne Nielsen 1842-1902

Tante Johanne and Her Family

The letters of Tante Johanne and her family provide a poignant insight into the life and hardships of one immigrant woman of the broad reaches of the upper Midwest. That woman is Johanne Nielsen, and this is her story.

Although Johanne emigrated from Denmark as a young woman, she never felt at home in America. Instead, her life was pervaded by a persistent loneliness and a deep desire to return to her native land. Because that longing for Denmark was paralleled by a craving for spiritual assurance and fellowship, the hardships which she experienced and that are reflected in these letters are more mental and spiritual than physical.

That she experienced the physical hardships associated with other immigrant women is certain: the burden of housework and childbearing, chores and illness, severe weather and crop failure, financial difficulties and death. These hardships, however, seldom loom large in the letters. Instead, they lurk between the lines and behind the scene. Rather it is her insatiable longing for spiritual nurture and fellowship with other Danes and her yearning for Denmark and what it represented that were her greatest hardships. Here was a soul that would be restless until at last it found eternal rest.

If this is the story of Johanne Nielsen, it is also the story of her family. Her husband, except for his frequent illnesses, does not play a large role in the letters. The daughters, especially Carol, Julia and Gertrude, however, stand out as enterprising and ambitious young women. The sons, often assisted by their sisters, perform the arduous but necessary work on their Iowa farm where they eventually prosper. As such they were typical of many immigrant families.

Johanne and her husband Herman Nielsen left Denmark in the early 1870s. They had three daughters, Laurine, Marie (Mae) and Carol, at the time. They settled first in Streator, Illinois, but then in the mid-eighties moved on to Algona, Iowa. Algona, however, could not hold the younger generation, and one after the other their daughters, who appear so impressively innovative and active in these letters, moved westward where they believed greater opportunity awaited them in Washington state.

During their years in Illinois, Johanne gave birth to seven more children, three girls, Julia, Gertrude and Ella, and four boys, Christof, Christian, Niels and Carl. Christof, her firstborn son, died while little more than an infant and was buried in what for Johanne must have been still a harsh and strange land. Her seventh daughter, Pauline, was born after the family had moved to Iowa.

Although she had one sister, Ane Kristine, living in Chicago, her stronger ties were with her family in Denmark where she had at least three sisters, Sidsel Marie, Maren,

1

and Ane Marie. The letters suggest she had other siblings. A Karen is mentioned in the letters but is not identified. Four of Ane Marie's sons, Christian, Viggo, Valdemar and Otto, came to the United States, but only Christian and Viggo remained permanently. These two sons took the name Mengers in America.

Christian, like his aunt and cousins, plays an important role in the narrative that unfolds in the letters. His full name was Niels Carl Christian Christiansen, but when he arrived in America in 1887, he took the name Mengers, the name of a Jewish child that his parents had sheltered in Denmark. After studying theology in Chicago, he was ordained as a pastor in the United Danish Evangelical Lutheran Church serving parishes in Illinois, Pennsylvania, Iowa, Montana, Missouri, Minnesota, and Wisconsin. He sensed that he was a participant in a significant aspect of history and very early began to collect and save letters and documents, both personal and general, that fell into his hands, organizing many of them by subject or writer. He inculcated this same sense of history and an awareness of the future importance of the seemingly commonplace in his daughter, Agathe Hansen, and his granddaughter, Sara Hansen-Walter. These three individuals are primarily responsible for collecting and preserving the more than 12,000 letters and other materials now comprising the Hansen-Mengers Collection in the Danish Immigrant Archive - Dana College. It is from that collection that the letters in this volume come. In fact, about half of them were located in a packet carefully marked in Christian Mengers' small, clear script: "Letters from my Tantes Johanne and Ane Kristine."

The letters of Johanne and her daughters exhibit an interesting generation difference. Carol, even as an early adolescent, reveals her desire to become fully Americanized when she writes in the first letter that although her name is Nielsine Caroline "that is Carrie in English." Later she chooses to be called Carol and often calls herself Nelson, using an anglicized form of the family's surname. Johanne, however, firmly remains Danish, signing her name invariably "Johanne Nielsen." Carol and her sisters forget whatever Danish they once may have known, writing all of their letters in English. Johanne, on the other hand, writes only in Danish . Perhaps she never learned to speak English which would have made neighborly contacts almost impossible and would have further increased her loneliness.

With this letter Carol introduces herself and her family to her cousin Christian (C.C. Mengers) who is still in Denmark. In the letter she reveals that she was the last of Johanne and Herman Nielsen's children to be born in Denmark and that the family has moved from Streator, Illinois to Algona, Iowa. The Americanization of the children is already evident.

Algona, Iowa
January 26, 1887

Our cousin Christian,

Since I have not yet heard from you in a long time, I will write to you. Now I will tell you how many we are in our family. We are nine children. The oldest is Laurine, the next Barbara Marie and after her, me, Nielsine Caroline, but that is Carrie in English. I was the youngest when we were in Denmark, then Julia, then Dena (Gertrude) and then the oldest boy, Christian, then Niels and Carl, and then little Ella the last.

Laurine is 19 years old, Marie is 16 and I am 15 and Julia 12 and Dena 9 and Christian 7 and Niels is 6 today and Carl 4 and little Ella 2 years old. Here are all the children, but there is a little boy dead. He was 16 months when he died. He would have been 10 years old if he had lived and his name is Christof. Then there are mother and father. That is the whole family. I still go to school; Marie works; Laurine is in Streator. We wish that she could study for something, but her boyfriend will not be without her.

We wish that you would send us your picture; we would like to see you. We would be glad if you could come over here soon. Now I must go to bed, but I am sure that you will write us as soon as you can. Greetings from all of us.

Write soon.

[Unsigned, but by Carol]

This is a photograph of the young Christian Mengers taken before he left Denmark in 1887.

4

Johanne uses a familiar Danish salutation at the beginning of this letter and reveals that her nephew (C.C. Mengers) is considering immigrating to the United States. Although parts of the letter are illegible, she reports that Herman has returned to Streator and is spending the winter there.

Algona, Iowa
January 26, 1887

Dear sisterson (Christian),

I was so glad when I got your letter because it has been so long since we have heard from you, but I do not blame you for not writing us sooner, we do not even deserve to hear from you! You write that you might come over here in the spring, we would be delighted to have you and then we could hear from all our relatives at home. You will probably find it difficult in the beginning but if you can only get a job then you will soon learn the language and then it is an easy thing.

Here are not many Danes. There is a family near us. They are the only Danes who have arrived. There are many Swedes though. I often go to the Swedish church. I can understand most of it.

Herman left for Streator on the 15th of August. I am very busy with all the children with the exception of Laurine; she stayed in Streator when we left to come out here. She would not travel out here because of her betrothed. Now she keeps house for her (father in Ranson?).

We would be very grateful if you could send us your portrait. I received your brother Niels' portrait sent (from Grimskov?), but there was no letter from him. I (illegible) that was before I received sister Annekerstine's (Ane Kristine) letter, but I could not. I think he looks like your father. But I could not thank him for it.

One of the girls will write; the boys are still too small. I shall now end my writing and thank you so much for the letter to us and promise to write you again soon.

Dearest greetings from me, and from all of our children.

Your aunt,

Johanne Nielsen

Daily Activity
of Immigrant Women

Although Johanne Nielsen writes," I have not had time to answer it (Christian's letter) because I am alone with the work," there is no indication of what that work consists, no mention of starting the fire on cold mornings, baking bread, gathering eggs, doing the laundry, and all those other repeated chores indoors and out that were the responsibility of the rural farm wife. One, however, can assume that her days were similar to those of other immigrant women such as Karen Miller, another Danish woman, who kept a journal of her activities about the same time on a farmstead in southern Minnesota. Excerpts from her entries for three successive days in January of 1894 may well give some idea of how Johanne spent her time.

"January 28 A snowfall during the morning hours. Peter and Karl did the milking themselves, and I began my work in the house by baking a cake, because Father and Peter are going to Henry Peter Nielsen with something for him. He is sick with pneumonia. While they were gone, I made a cheese and I baked both white bread and brown bread. When they came home, we had our supper. Karl had been at school but returned at the same time. I was glad when they came for I had not been very well today, but God be praised that I am not worse off. I thank you, my Heavenly Father, for every day that you give me and that you permit me to live through your mercy. Protect me every day to my end in faith and trust in you. Amen.

"January 29 Good weather. All three are at school. Father is at the creamery. I am washing and baking. I thought that I would bake some cookies also, but I feel so tired. Father has gone to Hammernes this evening. I will then stop for today and lie down to rest in Jesus' name with thanks for the day that has now ended never again to return, but it is recorded with the Heavenly Father. Forgive me also for the sins committed this day and let them never again come to mind. This I ask you in the name of Jesus. Amen.

"January 30 Very fine weather. We can even go without mittens. All three are at school. I am baking cookies and otherwise doing the regular housework. Jens and Rasmus and Johannes Evolsen were here for dinner. This afternoon I have been sewing a little. . . " (Miller 11-12).

Not only do these three entries give some idea of Karen Miller's daily activities, but they also indicate that Johanne Nielsen's spiritual sensitivities were common to other Danish immigrant women.

6

Internal evidence suggests that this letter belongs to the autumn of 1887. Christian has arrived in Chicago, but Johanne is unable to encourage him to come to Algona to find work because of the difficult times.

[Undated, but autumen1887]
Dear sisterson (Christian),

We received your letter awhile ago and learned from it that you are in Chicago. I know that it is not right of us that we have not written you long ago. I have wanted to do it every night but I just never got around to it. (illegible.) We have received your picture and portrait, and we are so pleased with it. I do not know how to express how thankful I am. (illegible.)

We are all fairly well, and we have had a good harvest this summer. Now the worst thing is that the house is too small. There is not room for all of us because now all the children, with the exception of Marie, are home. We are not very eager about making additions to the house because we do not know if we will have the house next year. We will probably have to get a house in town for some of us until we get another farm. (illegible.)

We are very sorry to hear that you cannot get a good job, but this is how it usually is when you first get here. We cannot ask you to come out here to work because during the winter there is not one single day of work and the winter is very long. I only wish that we could meet out here in the summer. Perhaps we can arrange it so that we will need you, or perhaps there will be something else available for you. This summer it has been very hard to find work.

I wrote your parents awhile ago, but I do not think they have received the letter yet. If you hear from them will you please, in your next letter, let us know how they are?

The fondest greeting from all of us, both big and small. Let us know how you are doing. If you decide to stay in Chicago I am afraid that the letter with the address you asked for, will not come because I sent it a long time ago.

The dearest greetings from me,

Your aunt,

Johanne Nielsen.

Tante Johanne characteristically crowded additional messages in the margins of her letters. Her sentences ran together, her spelling was unreliable, and her penmanship was sometimes illegible.

At this point there is a five-year gap in the correspondence preserved in the archives, but the tone of this letter suggests continued contact. The letter offers interesting insight into the travel and communication of the day. Travelers must have stopped at the post office for possible messages.

Algona, Iowa
August 28, 1892

Mr. N. C. C. Christiansen Mengers
Algona, Iowa

Dear cousin (Christian),

We received your letter last evening.

We are very much pleased to hear that you are coming to see us.

If we had the slightest idea when you were coming, we would meet you at the train. But I am afraid you have already reached Algona. We will look all over town for you today. And if we do not find you, we will leave our address.

Your cousin,

Sena (Carol)

Our address is:

Herman Nelson
5 miles east of Algona

You can ask for Mr. Julius Pleth. He is our agent and nearly everybody knows where to find him. If you do not find him, then go to Bangdon and Hudson's Grocery store and they will direct you. Their store is on the south side of Main St., one block west of the P.O.

Hyrderøsten

Jeg er den gode Hyrde; den gode Hyrde sætter sit Liv til for Faarene. Joh. 10, 11.

for denne lader Dørvogteren op, og Faarene høre hans Røst. Joh. 10, 3.

Hver den, som er af Sandheden, hører min Røst.
Joh. 18, 37.

4de Aarg.   Chicago, Ill., den 5. November 1892.   Nr. 21.

„Herren vor Retfærdighed!"

Nu Lov og Pris! jeg ved ej mer',
  Som staar tilbage — alt er færdigt.
Hvad helst hos mig jeg føler, ser,
  Er Lammet dog den Ære værdigt,
At det for mig har sonet alt
Og tusendfold for mig betalt —
    Alt, ja, alt.

Jeg er vist ej tilfreds med mig;
  Thi i mit Kjød bo Synder alle;
Mit Hjærte bær' endnu i sig
  Det gamle Æbles bitre Galde.
Hvi synger jeg dog glad og fro
Om evig Raade, Fred og Ro —
    Glad og fro?

Det har jeg, Jesus! blot af dig;
  Du, du er værdig Frydesangen,
    dit dyre Blod for mig
      Gud indgangen.

De Saar nu raabe hver en Stund,
  De raabe højt om Sejersstriden;
De raabe: Naade og Miskund
  For alle Adams Børn i Tiden!
Saa staar du, Jesus, og for mig
Hos Gud, „en Præst evindelig"—
    Og for mig.

Naar jeg er skrøb'lig, kold og svag,
  Adspredt af alt, som møder Øje,
Da har jeg en, som Nat og Dag
  Min Talsmand er hist i det høje,
Som for Guds Aasyn staar for mig
Og udi alt fremstiller sig
    Selv for mig.

Naar jeg er kold, saa er han varm,
  Er jeg adspredt, er han andægtig;
Naar jeg er syndig, svag og arm
  Da er han hellig, ren, almægtig.
Blot Skrøb'lighed har jeg i mig;
Min Hellighed har han i
    Ja, i sig

Hyrderøsten was the religious paper printed in Danish that is referred to frequently in Tante Johanne's letters.

10

Danish Publications
in the United States

Immigrants, uprooted not only from family and friends but also from their former homeland with its familiar language and ways, longed for communication. The emergence of an ethnic press, therefore, was an inevitable occurrence in the United States almost from its very inception. The Danes were no exception to this phenomenon.

Although a few Danes had come to America in the colonial era, by and large, the Danish immigration to the United States was later and smaller than that from Norway and Sweden. This explains why most of the early publications with which the Danes were associated were joint Scandinavian ventures primarily with the Norwegians whose language and attitudes were so similar to those of the Danes. In her thorough study of the Danish language press in the United States, Marion Marzolf states, "The immigrants founded 34 Danish-language and 24 Dano-Norwegian newspapers in the three previous decades, but only 15 remained as 1900 began" (Marzolf 117). These fifteen papers represented two basic types. Some, like _Den Danske Pioneer_ (The Danish Pioneer), _Bien_ (The Bee), _Revyen_ (The Review), _Nordlyset_ (The Northern Light), and _Ugebladet_ (The Weekly) were general newspapers covering a wide range of subjects - local, national and worldwide. Others like _Dannevirke_, named for the Danish border fortification in Slesvig, _Danskeren_ (The Dane), and _Bikuben_ (The Beehive) were church-affiliated with a much heavier coverage of church news. _Dannevirke_ was the publication of the Grundtvigian Lutherans; _Danskeren_, of the United Danish Lutherans; and _Bikuben_, of the Mormons.

There is no evidence in the letters, however, that Herman and Johanne Nielsen subscribed to any of these leading Danish papers with the exception of _Danskeren_, but we do know that they read _Hyrderøsten_ (The Shepherd's Voice). Whether they subscribed to this religious publication or whether C. C. Mengers sent occasional issues to them cannot be determined. This paper, however, published by C. C.'s mentor, P. C. Trandberg, was exactly what Johanne craved.

The masthead of _Hyrderøsten_ contained three verses from the Gospel of John: " I am the good shepherd. The good shepherd lays down his life for the sheep" (10:11). "For him the gatekeeper opens the door, and the sheep hear his voice" (10:13). "Everyone who is of the truth hears my voice" (18:37). Over these verses appeared the title of the publication and a picture of Jesus as the Good Shepherd in a medallion surrounded by flowers.

Hyrderøsten appeared semi-monthly and was published first in Chicago and then later in Minneapolis. Its subscription rate for a year was sixty cents but for subscrip-

11

tions to Denmark, Slesvig or Norway the rate was eighty-five cents! In keeping with the religious persuasion of its editor, P.C. Trandberg, the publication professed to be an Evangelical Free Church Paper.

A perusal of the contents of the November 5, 1892 issue, which might be the one that Johanne Nielsen refers to in her December letter, indicates that it included three poems, twelve articles, and an acknowledgement of and thank you for a cash contribution to Trandberg's school for pastors in Chicago.

Some of the articles were of a theological nature such as the conclusion of N. Th. Ylvisaker's "The Law and the Gospel," Trandberg's "Did Luther Foresee a Free Church and a Living Congregation," and a discussion of the Christian's position on war and peace. Most of the articles, however, were short, inspirational pieces for the general reader with such titles as "Clouds," "A Donkey in the Ditch" and " The Flowers' Testimony." It is likely that these latter articles were the ones that Johanne found most meaningful. The contents of the paper, however, were not exclusively religious. References in the letters make it clear that at times Hyrderøsten carried helpful remedies and practical hints for everyday life.

Left: P.C. Trandberg, the editor of Hyrderøsten, was Christian Mengers' religious mentor. He also married Christian and Dorthea.

Right: Gothuldine Trandberg, daughter of Danish Baron Luttieaux, promoted her husband's views after his death.

At the beginning of this letter Johanne reveals her deep spiritual longings and her appreciation for the religious publications that Christian has sent them. His actions are an indication of his religious fervor and of the rather common practice of distributing tracts to friends and strangers alike. She also makes mention of the daughters' preparation for teaching and of the Danish paper <u>Hyrderøsten</u> (The Shepherd's Voice). A major concern for her, of course, is Herman's health. All of these subjects will appear often in the letters. It is evident that Christian's brothers, Valdemar and Viggo, together with the former's wife, Laura, have arrived in America. The letter shows how much photographs are cherished by theses immigrants who seldom saw one another.

Algona, Iowa
October 23, 1892

Dear Christian,

It is a while since we got your welcome letter and the good Scripture (tract) you sent. Thank you so much for them. I have read them many times, and I got Herman to read the little book, but that was not testimonial enough for me. I read it aloud to all of them one evening. I am glad to hear you have so many meetings and edification sessions. I think so often if I could be there to hear the many good words spoken in Danish, I would be better. I think how great it is to be part of the host of brothers and sisters going to our home. But we need to be satisfied to be where our Lord has set us. I hope and pray that our good God will gather us all in a little crowd to praise our God and Savior.

Julia is home and sends her greetings. She likes being where she is, but time is short. She has two or three weeks left, and then she hopes to go to normal (school) this winter with her money, and Sine (Carol) will help her a little. Sine is busy. She is taking examinations this week. She will thank you herself for all the tracts you sent. She will write. Greet Valdemar and his wife and thank them for the photographs. They are beautiful and we are happy to get them. When we get new pictures taken, we will remember you. We hope to have one from you and Viggo before too long.

Herman has been very sick but is better. He could not even move for a week. He was spitting blood and I was afraid he never would get well. We never know when the Lord will call us. I talked to him about the one thing needful from a full heart, and brought him to the throne of mercy in my prayers. Christian, pray for him and for us all. It was so lonely here when you left. I now have no one to talk to about heavenly things, but then I turn to my dear

Savior who will comfort me in my loneliness and strengthen me in my faith till the end.

Loving greetings from all of us, big and little, but most from

Your aunt,

Johanne Nielsen.

When you write to your parents, greet them from me and ask them to write a little letter to me. I long to hear from them.

I have not tried the medicine for Herman. I looked for it in <u>Hyrderøsten</u> but it was not there.

This letter provides an insight into the conditions and loneliness of young rural school teachers living and boarding away from home. Without any means of transportation, they, like their students, had to walk to and from school every day regardless of the weather. The letter also indicates that Christian's brother, Valdemar, and his wife have had a baby. This was their first daughter, and she was named Leah. Carol also expresses concern for her parents' financial well-being. She is convinced that it is only if her sisters also become teachers will they be able to provide them much needed assistance. The letter strikes a poignant note as it approaches its end but then concludes with a prayer for her two cousins who are preparing themselves for the Lutheran ministry.

Elmore, Minnesota
November 22, 1892

Dear cousin Carl (Christian),

I rec'd your books and cards. I thank you very much for them, I will have time enough now to read them all. I have not had time for anything before examination. Now I am teaching in the north part of our county. I have only two miles to Minnesota. That is the reason I get mail in Elmore, Minnesota. I have a nice little school. But I have nearly two miles to walk and a river to cross which has no bridge over it. The ice cracks every time I cross, but everybody is so kind to me, I think I can stand it all the term. I get very lonely, and wish I were back to school or at home but we must all endure something hard. So I try to be contented.

How are cousin Walter (Valdemar) and his wife and baby getting along? And how does Viggo like school? I suppose you and he are very busy, but I wish you would write me a long letter and tell me all about them all.

I cannot tell you very much about home as I have not heard from home since I left, which is two weeks ago. But they were all well then.

Julia is going to attend the same school that I did. If nothing has happened she has commenced last week. I am glad she can go. I think the only way we girls can ever do anything for father, is to teach school. I get 28 dollars per month. I hope Julia can teach next winter too.

But you must not think that I think of nothing but this world for I do. I am glad you spoke as you did when you were out here. You have done my little mother good.

Now, dear cousin, I must close my letter as it is growing late. My little children have been home for quite a while and I feel lonely in the school house all alone.

Do write to me soon! I am so lonely and a letter from anyone does me good. I pray that God's blessing may rest on you and Vega (Viggo) and that you both may become ministers of the Gospel. Now good by.

Your loving cousin,

Carol Nelson.

P.S. Give my regards to all of my cousins.

After a reference to being very busy and to some of her usual themes, this letter discloses the difficult economic conditions confronting American farmers in the early 1890's.

Algona, Iowa
December 11, 1892

Dear Christian,

You shall have many thanks for your much welcomed letter. I received it a while ago. I have not had the time to answer it because now I work alone. Gertrude and Ella and all three boys go to school every day.

Yesterday Herman and I went in to town. We talked with Julia. She asked me to greet you many times. She said she will write you soon, but she studies so hard that she stays up almost the whole nights. I am afraid that she does more than she can actually stand. Sine's (Carol) school is near Minnesota.

Herman is a little better than he has been. He has not tried the medicine that was in the <u>Hyrderøsten</u> because we do not think it is a chest illness but rather that it comes from the head. He takes medicine for it, and we think it helps.

This year is a hard winter for us. There was nothing to sell but some pigs and a little hay. The cattle prices are so low that it does not help us to sell them. There are plenty of them.

Kind regards to you from all of us. Greet both your brothers and your brother's wife from us. How is their little girl?

If it were not because it is so far, I would be there to visit you. Write soon.

From your aunt,

Johanne Nielsen

The Rural School

When three of Herman and Johanne Nielsen's daughters decided to become teachers, they entered one of the few professions that was open to women in the late nineteenth and early twentieth centuries. Women had moved into the ranks of rural school teachers during the Civil War to take the place of young men volunteering to serve in the contending armies. Their position "gave them status in the community, educational opportunities, and wages enough to sustain themselves" (Fuller 160). By the time the war was over their status as teachers was secure largely because local school boards soon discovered that they could hire women on the average of ten dollars less per month than men. Thus both a profession and a practice of lower salaries were established for women, but certainly these daughters when they joined the ranks of approximately 200 rural school teachers in Kossuth County, Iowa, (History) even with lower salaries, had made professional advancement that would very likely not have been open to them in Denmark.

The letters indicate that the Nielsen daughters worked hard to get their teaching certification. Whether they studied at a state normal school, at a teacher institute, or as a part of a normal training program in a local high school is not clear from the letters. Iowa, it appears, offered all three types of training in the 1890's but the fact that the girls remained rather close to home suggests that their training was either in an institute or at a local high school. In any case, the daughters not only received their Iowa credentials but they went on to receive certification in Washington state and at least Gertrude also taught in Alaska.

The schoolhouses in which the Nielsen sisters taught very likely conformed to Fuller's description of the typical Midwestern one-room schoolhouse: ". . . it was a rectangular frame structure, almost invariably painted white, with three windows on each of its longer sides, one door squarely in the middle of its shorter side, and a small belfry directly above the door" (Fuller 72).

Writers who attended rural schools retained vivid recollections of the experience. Almost a half-century after the event, Hamlin Garland recalled the Iowa school he attended, "The school-house which was to be the center of our social life stood on the bare prairie about a mile to the southwest, and like thousands of other similar buildings in the west, had not a leaf to shade it in summer nor a branch to break the winds of a savage winter" (Garland 95). Sophus Keith Winther has the Grimsen boys going to a school that "was located at a crossroads on a piece of land about one hundred yards square. The yard was surrounded by thorn trees and a heavy growth of weeds covered the playground up to the door of the school house. No farmer ever took the time to run a mower over the playground, but in time the weeds would be trampled down and a space cleared for ball games in the fall and for fox and geese after the snow had come" (Winther 141).

Unlike the modern American school year consisting of two terms of approximately four and one-half months each, the school year of the rural school district of the late nineteenth and early twentieth centuries was determined by farm work. This meant that terms were short and avoided the busy seasons of fall harvest, spring field work, and summer haying. Not only were terms short, but teachers were often changed, sometimes, as the letters reveal, even during a term. Because of the demand for help in the field, it was normal that the winter term when farm work was at a standstill had the largest enrollment. "During the winter and up till the beginning of spring work on the farm," Winther writes, "there were about forty children at the Laurel Hope School" (Winther 141). Many of these were fifteen, sixteen and seventeen year old boys, bigger than their teacher but doing the work of fourth graders because of their fragmented studies.

An article in <u>The Educational Review</u> of December 1896 describes those studies as being "chiefly a course of study in the school arts, reading, writing, arithmetic and English grammar, together with book-geography and a little United States history" (Swett 124). The respective roles of teacher and students in pursuing these studies is succinctly stated by a nineteenth century educator: "It was the office of the teacher to keep order and hear recitations. It was the duty of pupils to memorize textbook lessons and recite them without note, comment, or question" (Swett 121). So important was order that the same educator advises the teacher, "Secure order, if possible, without corporal punishment; but secure obedience at all hazards" (Swett 178).

Besides keeping order and hearing recitations, the rural school teacher had to perform every janitorial function that might arise, from cleaning the floors, washing the blackboards, making and maintaining the fire and shovelling the snow, to doing minor repairs on school property and a score of other unexpected tasks. Thus it was no mean undertaking that the Nielsen daughters assumed when they began teaching in their rural schools that represented some of Iowa's nearly fourteen thousand small schools. More than twenty-five hundred of these had an average daily attendance of less than ten students each in 1900 (Fuller 129).

Whatever the shortcomings of the rural school and whatever difficulties the teachers faced, something significant must have been achieved because Iowa had the second highest literacy rate in the nation in 1880, and by 1900 she tied Nebraska for first place among all the states (Fuller 130).

It is evident from this letter that Julia is romantically attracted to her seminarian cousin and wishes to win his favorable attention as she describes her studies, her work, and her reading. One wonders what simple flirtations were the bases for her "naughtiness."

Algona, Iowa
December 24, 1892

My dear cousin Christ,

I received the letter you sent me through Mr. Bidgood before you went back to Chicago. But Christ I really have not had time to write to you before. I did not stay at Mr. Potters as long as I had expected to, as school commenced November 7, and Carol was bound I should go the first term. I have now gone eight weeks. We have only two weeks more school this term, then we will have one day's vacation, and then school commences again on Monday. Carol is going to try and keep me at the Normal two terms more, and then I am going to try teacher's examination. Christ, have you ever had your breakfast served since you went away as I used to serve it when you was with us? Well, I cannot blame you for wanting to rest as much as possible, if you study as hard as I do. I never retire until two or three o'clock in the night. They give us so long lessons that it takes us nearly all night to get them, and I will not think of such a thing as going to school without my lessons. Well, even if I must study hard, and stay up late, I like school best of every thing.

Have you had examinations? And how does your brother like the school?

Christ, I have not forgotten what a naughty girl I was the last evening I was at home, have you? I have often thought of it, and wondered if you have, hoping that you have forgotten all about it. I will venture to say that I am sorry I was so naughty (but I suppose you know that it is natural for me to be so). Christ, I have read some of the books you sent Carol, but have not had time to read them all yet, but will as soon as I can.

Well Christ, I came home yesterday and so I washed today and have written a letter to Washington this evening, so I am tired. Hoping you will forgive me for not writing to you before, I remain,

Your naughty cousin,

Julia Nelson

Love from all to you and both of your brothers, and a kiss from me to your little niece. Good by. Write soon.

Julia

P. S. Mamma got a letter from your papa yesterday. They are all well, and aunt Maren is just the same as she has been for so long.

And we had a letter from cousin Fanny also. She has a little baby girl, two months old.

Well it is midnight and I must go to bed.

Do not forget to kiss that baby for me.

Throughout his life Christian kept copies of certain letters that he wrote. These were letters the contents of which he was especially pleased or were ones that he first wrote out in his native Danish and then translated into English, sending the translation to the intended recipient, This letter represents both reasons; the letter on page 45, the first. Christian is responding to Carol's lonely note written from the empty school-house. He misunderstands the nature of her loneliness and makes his response a treatise on spiritual salvation and abandonment. In this letter is revealed both the positive and negative aspects of the Inner Mission of the Danish Lutheran Church. On the one hand, there is deep faith, personal commitment to God and Christ Jesus, and concern for the spiritual well-being of others; on the other hand, there is a disregard for the sensitivities of others, the use of pressure tactics, and the over dramatizations of language and events. The letter concludes with family news.

Chicago, Illinois
December 29, 1892

Dear cousin Carol,

Thank you for your highly welcome letter, and I apologize for not answering earlier. I have been very busy with Christmas, so I have not been able to write till now. I was sick Christmas Eve. Now I am fairly well again and I will now answer your dear letter. So, you have started work with the little ones. May it not only influence their brains but also their hearts. Then God will bless you and the children in his time. It must be very rough and cold out there both in the old house at home and at your house, but I am glad that people treat you well because that softens and warms the heart and it is from the heart that all life flows out.

It seems to me that nothing is as boring as an empty schoolhouse. I have often sat in an empty schoolhouse, just like you did when you wrote your letter to me, and it has always brought thoughts about the emptiness of life to my mind, and then I have often, when I thought everything was lonely and empty inside of me and around me, bent my knees in quiet prayer to Him, who is the only one who can bring happiness and joy where there used to be the opposite inside my heart, my soul and mind, and then it was as if the house was full of everything that was dear to us because the glory of God fills it. You say "You must not think that I think of nothing but this world." I do not think so!

I think you as well think a great deal about your soul, and for that I thank my God, but we must renounce the world and turn to God, to our dear Savior. Imagine that a dear friend took you in his arms when you were very little, before you even understood yourself how dear you were to him, and as you grew up he was always near, and without you knowing it, whenever dangers threatened you, he would put his protecting hands over you.

But the time came when you began to understand that he had followed you all your days and unnoticed been near you in good and bad. You might have realized that it was so, but even though it obviously grieved him each time you exposed yourself to danger, you did not consider that, but kept running from one danger to another to meet a vague aspiration within, so that you in your blind hurry did not understand that you could only find satisfaction by giving yourself up to him who loved you with an eternal love.

Then suddenly on your pilgrimage through life you felt overwhelmed by a heavy burden and faintness brought on alone by all the dangers that you had endured. You felt ill and helpless, but yet you saw immediately what you have never noticed before. In front of you a yawning gulf, a deep river, you stand right on the brink - to your right a ravenous lion - to your left a flaming fire, behind you only a narrow path of where all the difficulties you so far have had are piled up like an insurmountable high mountain. Imagine there you stand! What will you do? If you go to the right, you will be swallowed by the jaws of the lion, and if you go to the left, you will be engulfed by the flames, and if you go back, yes! You can try to get over the high mountain; but never, never will you succeed. If you continue, you will fall down into the jaws of the lion in your deadly fatigue, because remember the path is so narrow. Death, death, death, and death, in all 4 directions. Then where will I turn? Then imagine that your matted glazed eyes looked at the river in front of you, you caught a glimpse of your trusty friend on the other side of the river, you hear his voice as a mild quiet whisper: Throw yourself out! Trust me. I will save you.

You doubt, no! no! You believe and throw yourself into the river - and once again you feel the embrace of your never failing friend. Now you are saved on the other side on the light shore of bliss, now you realized how great his love for you was, because he abandoned himself to the waves of death to save you, and first now you see that he was with you and you with him. Danger-free shore - does that then mean no danger anymore? Oh yes! See, here is also the lion and the fire - here are also mountains, but now you have your friend who is stronger than all of this and you know that he loves you. But the lion is the worst, imagine: it comes like an affectionate cat and rubs its head against you whispering: I will not hurt you anymore. Think now, this lion is your friend's worst enemy and he, your friend, knows what will happen to you if you believe in and listen to his enemy's flattery. Think about his love - then think could you really live in confidence with first him and then with his enemy? Oh no! Such things are not possible. No! You would live entirely for your rescuer, entirely for your friend, entirely for your Savior. You know this is how we are brought to our Savior, the sacrament of baptism, but despite his protecting love, we do not appreciate what he was to us and the whole world, we wander in sin during our adolescence without recognizing his love. But when we realize how lost in sin we are. Yes! That time will come. Happy if it comes to us while it is still the time of grace. Consciousness of sin often knocks on our door, but few are those who let it in, but in it will, and woe unto us if it first occurs in eternity. Then when it comes it is like a big mountain. Thousands of people will not admit that their sins are insurmountable and therefore they try to climb the mountain, all with the force of their own stubbornness, but it will fail and they will sink down to eternal perdition! No! There is only rescue in one way and that is, when one has realized one is lost, to throw oneself with confidence and faith into the river of mercy and get washed white in Jesus' reconciliating river of blood and feel secure in the arms of Jesus. And then one cannot love the world or the things that are in it, because then we will only love our Savior, all our love will be for Him, because we cannot serve two Lords. Now back to the beginning - I do not think that you only think about the world, no - not at all! But I hope that you with God's grace will understand what I have written here, that it is important to depart entirely from the world, the devil, death and sin and live entirely for our dear Savior. Oh, dear Carol, surrender to him who in both life and death can make you happy and blessed. But is it urgent? Is there not plenty of time? Oh no! God wants us to use the pleasant time. Now - God is to be found. Just now in this very moment I realized how important it is to be ready.

Right here next to the house I live in they are now building a very big school-house. One man stood on a wood hauling wagon and then there was one man on each floor by a window. They handed the boards from one to the other, from the wagon and all the way up to the top floor. But one board suddenly broke in two and fell down from the 3rd floor and as the man on the wagon looked up he got the end of the board right in his forehead. He fell down between the horses and the wagon. I left the letter and rushed out and we carried him into our house where it was warm until the police wagon came to take him home to his wife and small children. He did not understand the message of Jesus - poor man! But bleeding and in pain as he was, miserable and despicable, still he had a curse on his lips, he clung desperately to my hand and asked us to help him, but Jesus he did not need. It appeared that his forehead was crushed. Whether he lives or dies I do not know; but he has neglected the pleasant time so now he cannot seek God! Oh yes! It is urgent, since we do not know what will happen to us from morning to evening.

Dear Carol, do you remember what you said one evening at home? You said: "Mother, if this is the way, you go ahead and I will follow." Your mother has found the way! found that Jesus is the way, the truth and the life. Have you followed her on the hard way? You asked me to write a long letter, and this is long so I will end. Dear greetings to you from my brothers Viggo and

Valdemar and his wife. Their little baby is so cute. I am so glad for it and they themselves are thankful to God for it.

Yes, Viggo and I must study very hard. A couple of months ago I got a letter from our cousin Laurine Longowsky, when she was home in Streator. I have heard from other Danes that she has had a little baby, I do not know if it is true. Valdemar got a letter from home from sister Ane, who tells that aunt Maren is very ill. I do not remember who of you girls it was who needed Lina Petersen's address; but if it was you, here it is: 687 Armitage Ave, Chicago, Ill.

I got a letter from my dear little aunt Hanne (Johanne) 14 days ago which made me very happy. Greet her and uncle and everybody at home from me. Finally, I want to wish you a happy new year, may it be truly new year for you so you can live in the name of Jesus, I believe it will! So goodbye with dearest greetings from

Your affectionate cousin,

Christian

The Inner Mission Movement

Johanne Nielsen and her nephew Christian Mengers obviously reflect the position of the Inner Mission movement in Denmark that was especially influential in the United Danish Evangelical Lutheran Church of America, formally organized in Minneapolis, Minnesota, in 1896. The leader of the Inner Mission in Denmark was Vilhelm Beck (1829-1901). The movement, which reacted to what was perceived as the arid formalism of the Church of Denmark in the nineteenth century and the spiritual indifference of the people, asserted the Lutheran doctrine of the priesthood of all believers by inspiring Christian lay people to exert themselves on behalf of their faith. This lay people did first of all by forthrightly talking with one another about their faith - both their conviction of sin and their joyous realization that God had accepted them in Christ Jesus. But secondly, and equally important to them, was the desire to awaken "sleeping Christians" and attract them and others to a profoundly personal relationship to God in a living faith. Theodor I. Jensen in his essay " The Prairie Sod Was Hard: How Shall Personal Faith Commitment Be Nurtured?" states, "One of the main themes in the typical United Church sermon, thus, was the call to repentance and faith in the gospel. A second theme, virtually as important as the first, was the call to holiness of life before God"(Lutz 155).

These various emphases are certainly present in Johanne Nielsen's letters. A sincere concern for her family's spiritual well-being dominates her life, but to her credit she is aware that that very concern can so easily result in impatient nagging on her part. She, too, must grow in grace even as she seeks deeper spiritual awareness and joy for those whom she loves.

This undated letter appears to be from the spring of 1893. It describes Johanne's spiritual loneliness which cannot be satisfied by family alone. The companionship of fellow Christians is required, and in her case, the companionship of fellow Danes. After news of the family she expresses a desire for "a large elegant" Bible.

[Undated; Algona, Iowa]

Dear Christian,

It is a long time since I received your dear letter. Many thanks for it. I have read it many times to comfort me in my loneliness. You must think that I should not talk of loneliness when I have my husband and all my children around me, but honestly, Christian, I am lonesome. I think if I could only talk with a brother or sister in the Lord, I would have a lot to talk about. I know that Jesus Christ is to be our refuge and comfort in all our need. I will pray the dear Savior both early and late that He by His holy Spirit will strengthen me in my faith and give me patience, that He in His mercy will let His light shine into their hearts so they can understand how important it is for them to hear and read God's word and care for their soul's salvation. The time comes and goes, and the more I talk to them, the more impossible it seems. I see that my faith is too weak. I know the Almighty God can and will find a way for them when we have patience to wait for His time.

I will let you know how we are. We are all well. Herman is not strong, but is better than he was last summer. Carol is home after her school term was over. They were all glad for her up there and she will go back in a couple of weeks for the second term. Julia has begun the last term of normal if Carol can keep her there so that Julia can get her certificate in the fall. The girls send greetings and would love to hear from you, but it is hard to write when one constantly has to study. Julia studies almost harder than she is able to stand. She sits up half the night and I often worry but she is well and likes to study. Greet your brothers and Valdemar's wife, and thank Viggo for the card he sent. I was hoping for a letter, but of course he would not have time to write. We hope you are well again. You ask if we have a Bible. No, but maybe this summer. It will be expensive because I would like a large elegant one. Greetings most hearty from us all, but first and last from me.

Your aunt,

Johanne Nielsen

Write as soon as you can. We all long to hear from you. Goodbye. Live well in the Lord.

HAN 988 3-1-12 Danish   27

Christian has obviously sent Johanne a Bible. Whether or not it was the elegant Bible she desired, she is very grateful for it. The letter reveals that Otto, a third brother of Christian, has come to the United States but will return to Denmark whence Johanne longs to accompany him. Whether Karen Marie is a niece of Johanne's or a sister has not been determined. Her sister Maren, however, has long been ill. In the intervening years Laurine has married her fiance and moved west to Washington. Marie, who is also in Washington, is engaged.

Algona, Iowa
September 14, 1893

Dear Christian,

For a long time I have wanted to answer your letter, but we have had house guests every day for the last 8 days so it has not been possible for me to write.

First of all I want to thank you many times for the Bible and for the little song book; it was the dearest and best present that I could get. Then, thank you for your letter and card. I was very glad for them. I thought that you had left Chicago, but now I learn from your letter that you have not had that much time.

We would be glad to see you again. I hope that you soon will come out here. Cannot one of your brothers come with you?

Until you wrote, we did not know that Otto was over here. We have not heard from Denmark since January, but now I got a letter from Karen Marie a couple of days ago. They are all well. My poor sister Maren is still alive. I hope that our Lord will strengthen her in her hard illness and soon take her home to himself.

Now I will let you know how we are all doing. We are all well. Herman was much better this summer. We use the piece of advice that was in Hyrderøsten. I think it helps.

For the time being Sine (Carol) is home, but it will probably only be for fourteen days. Then she will go back to her school again. Julia has attended school in Swea City. Now she goes to normal for 10 weeks. Then she has the same school again. Sine is now teaching her second year. Gertrude is out to work. Christian and Niels have done all the field work this summer, and Carl and Ella have taken care of the cattle. Small grain was very bad. The corn was fairly good. It has been very dry this summer.

28

We got a letter from Washington fourteen days ago. Laurine now has 3 children. The last one is a little girl; she is one month old. Marie is engaged to a doctor. I still do not know if they will stay out there or if they will come here to Algona.

I will now end my writing this time in the hope that I soon will see you and talk to you, and I will remember that God's mercy and blessing will be with you and your work both where you are and where you go , that those who listen to the word of God will awaken from their " sleep of sin" and take care of their souls' salvation. Greet all your brothers from us. It is too bad that they do not have work. When will Otto travel home? If I only had the money, I would join him.

Julia wrote you a letter when she was teaching school, but you probably did not receive it yet. They are not at all offended that you have not written to them. They understand that there is no time for those who must study.

I have not yet sent money to <u>Hyrderøsten</u>; the subscription has run out. I hope you will continue to send it. I will send the money as soon as possible.

Kind regards to you from all of us, first and last from me.

Your aunt,

Johanne Nielsen

Farewell. Live well in the Lord.

Once again, thank you for what you sent.

Will you not write us and let us know when you are coming so we can pick you up in town? Julia is in Algona. You can ask for her; she rooms at Mr. Meknob.

Four of Tante Johanne's daughters who appear so prominantly in this book.
They are from top, left to right, Gertrude, Julia, Ella and Carol.
This picture dates from the time of the letters.

Based on Johanne's next letter, it is clear Julia has misdated this letter, writing 1893 instead of 1894. Not only does this letter report Carol's serious bout with typhoid fever, but it provides further interesting details about the role of the rural school teacher. Fannie is a mutual cousin and the daughter of their mother's sister, Ane Kristine.

Ledyard, Iowa
February 9, 1893

Rev. C. C. Mengers
232 Fairview Ave.
Chicago, Illinois

My dear cousin,

I suppose you think I have forgotten you. I have not but I have been so busy that I have hardly had time. Carol came up here to teach her school the first of October, taught one week then she was taken sick with typhoid fever. I came up here, and was going to teach her school until mine was to commence but Carol did not get well so I gave up my school and kept hers. She was sick up here 16 weeks, just went home 2 weeks tomorrow. I have been up here 18 weeks, but if all goes as it should my school will be out five weeks from today. I am so glad for it is so hard to teach this school. I have five boys that are larger than I, and two girls not quite as large as myself, beside the little ones.

I get $30 per mo. but I have not made much this winter as mama was up here 6 weeks and Gertrude 7, and I had to pay all our boards, and that amounted to $5 per week.

Well, cousin, how are they all getting along in Chicago? (I mean your brothers) and what are they doing? Where is cousin Fannie? I wrote to her quite awhile ago but she has not answered my letter. I went home last Saturday and came back Monday. They were all well then but I have not heard from home since.

Well, it is past 11 o'clock. I have written 4 letters so I am quite tired.

Give my love to all my cousins. Hoping to hear from you soon, I am

Your beloved cousin,

Julia Nelson

P. S. I must tell you how it is I happened to write to you this evening. I dreamed I saw you last evening, so I made up my mind to write to you this evening.

Good night,

Julia

PANIC OF 1893

When Johanne Nielsen writes about low farm prices and an over abundance of
livestock, she is not merely expressing a family or local condition but rather one that
characterized virtually the whole of American agriculture. Frederick Merk states,
"The twenty years 1877-97 were a period of ruinously low prices for farm produce,
of intense distress for farmers, not only for those in the United States but for farmers
elsewhere in the world" (Merk 473). The declining farm prices for the period are
indicated by the Department of Agriculture table reproduced by John D. Hicks in
the work The Populist Revolt (Hicks 56) which indicates that the price of wheat
dropped from $1.00 in 1878 to 63 cents in 1897, and that of corn from 43 cents to 29
cents. This was the average price and does not reflect the fact that the farther one
was from a railroad or from the market the lower the price was. Furthermore, the
prices listed included commissions to dealers and deductions for less than first class
grain besides being based on December figures which were generally higher. Most
farmers, in order to meet debts, were forced to sell earlier immediately after harvest
when the market was glutted and the prices much lower, and therefore rarely did the
farmers receive anything near the prices quoted. How ruinous the situation could be
is reflected in what may well be an extreme case by an agrarian agitator cited by
Hicks who complained of "eight cent corn, ten cent oats, two cent beef and no price
at all for butter and eggs" (Hicks 57).

The causes of this dismal agricultural picture were undoubtedly many, but certainly
among them was the spectacular expansion that occurred as a result of the Home-
stead Act of 1862, the significant extension of railroad lines to the trans-Mississippi
region, the availability of easy credit, and the influx of large numbers of European
immigrants all of which contributed to increased production. If this had been only a
national condition, worldwide market prices might have been sustained, but this
domestic expansion of agriculture occurred at the same time that rich farming areas
were being opened up in Canada, South America, and Australia. Furthermore
Sweden was experiencing several years of bumper crops of wheat. To complicate
matters further, European countries placed quarantines on American pork suspect-
ing it of being contaminated by trichinosis and hog cholera. A further blow to
American agiculture before the Panic of 1893 occurred when several years of
favorable weather were followed by a change in climatic conditions resulting in
unusually long and severe droughts beginning in the late 1880s (Merk 473-74).

A final blow not only to American agriculture but to the entire United States
economy was occasioned by what has become known as the Panic of 1893. According to Paul W. Glad, the New York Tribune reported in the summer of 1893, "The
failure of Schaffner & Co. and the Grant Locomotive Works at Chicago, the
Plankinton Bank at Milwaukee, the Victoria Cordage Company at Cinncinnati and
the Domestic Sewing Machine Company were each supposed to have liabilities
reckoned in the millions, beside 236 other failures in the United States alone, indicate

clearly the financial pressure" (Glad 71-72). Glad concudes that nearly 16,000 businesses and banks had failed by the end of the year and that there were 100,000 persons out of work in Chicago during the winter of 1893-1894 (Glad 72). When one considers that Chicago's population in 1900 was 1,698,575, then 100,000 unemployed would represent a very high percentage of the potential labor force of the city, especially when one realizes that families were large and that far fewer women worked outside of the home. No wonder that two of C. C. Mengers' brothers, Otto and Valdemar, became disillusioned with the "American dream" and returned to Denmark. Only C. C. and his youngest brother, Viggo remained in the United States. They may have been somewhat cushioned by the fact that they were not in the labor pool but rather divinity students. Severe as was the economic plight of the Danish immigrant, many of them longed for spiritual nurture and welcomed pastors of their faith into their midst. So C. C. and Viggo remained in the United States finding positions in churches that paid meager salaries.

This letter contains details of Carol's illness and slow recovery and indicates how tenderly the mother and sisters care for her. Herman became ill again which further complicated matters. The letter exudes with Johanne's spiritual concerns.

Algona, Iowa
February 8, 1894

Dear Chestian (Christian),

I have waited now so long for a letter from you and I long to hear how you are doing in Chicago. It is hard times all over.

 Now I will let you know how we are. Herman has been very ill this winter but now he is a little better again. Has Julia written to you? She was home for Christmas and she got your address. If she has not written, you probably have not heard how ill Sine (Carol) has been. Sine got a school about 40 miles from here at 30 dollars a month and Julia got one at 26 dollars a month. There were only two miles between where they lived. They were both happy because then they could spend time together. Sine started in early October and was to be there for six months, Julia's was for four months. When Sine had taught eight days, she got typhoid fever. Julia left immediately and got her to the doctor. The fever ceased after about one week and she got better. After 3 weeks she was able to sit up and the doctor promised her that she soon could go home and we waited for her every day. Anyway, the house where she stayed was very poor. Some of the windows were broken so she got a cold and then got a fever. Then Julia took Sine's school and let her own go. I had to go up and take care of Sine. I was there for 5 weeks. Then I got a letter that Herman was ill, so I went home and sent Gertrude up to take care of Sine. At that time Sine was so ill that we could not tell her that her father was ill; she could not understand why I had to leave her. She was so nervous. Every time we read a letter from home or from one of her sisters she would be so touched that she would faint! The doctor moved her to a better bed about one mile from here, there we have to pay 3 dollars per week even though Gertrude and I have worked a lot for them but this year is hard on everybody. However, this happened weeks ago in the middle of October. Now she is finally in Algona. She has been there for two weeks. We hope to get her home late this week. When she came to Algona, she could not walk by herself but now she can walk across the floor by herself. The reason why her illness is so long-lasting is that now her nerves are weakened. The costs of the doctor and the medicine and all the other things will be more than 75 dollars. But we should not fret over that but instead thank God for letting her live. When I was not sure how it would end, I prayed that God's will would be done and that it would serve us the best because I hope and believe that the good God with his wisdom gave her this illness to draw all of us closer to Him.

Yes, dear Christian, I pray at all hours that the mercy of God will help all of us realize that the vanity of this world is worth nothing and that our only aspiration should be the salvation of our souls and our heavenly home. God give us grace to do so for the sake of Jesus. Amen.

The rest of us are all well. Christian and Niels have almost done a piece of work and they go to school whenever it is possible. Julia is done with school in 5 weeks. It is hard for her but she manages very well but she must stay late every evening. There are some who go to the school who are older than she is. She is a good girl, every night after school she has walked one mile over to Sine and she gives Sine almost all the money she makes. If only Sine would be well again, then she would be satisfied. Julia has already been offered a position in another school in the spring for 4 months. The school is located 10 miles from here.

I know, dear Christian, that you do not have much time to write, but anyway I will ask you to write us a letter so we can hear how you are all doing. Greet Valdemar and his wife and little girl and your other brothers. Is Otto still there? Have you heard from Denmark? I long to hear from home and I wonder if my sister Maren is still alive!

Dearest greeting from all of us, first and last from me.

Your aunt,

Johanne Nielsen

Christian Mengers is depicted wearing his robe and ruff sometime following his ordination into the ministry of the United Danish Evangelical Lutheran Church.

Familiar subjects are treated in this letter, but at the end it becomes evident that Christian is either already engaged to or at any rate seriously interested in a "beloved." This young woman is Dorthea Henriksen of Hampton, Nebraska, who was working in Chicago at the time.

Algona, Iowa
March 11, 1894

Dear Chrestian (Christian),

Thank you so much for your highly welcomed letter. I waited so long for a letter from you and longed to hear how you are doing in Chicago. Then I wrote you a letter and I wrote the address which was in Hyrderøsten, but I put Chicago below, therefore I am afraid that you did not receive it. Julia wrote a letter to the same address.

If you have not received our letters you probably do not know that Sine (Carol) has been ill all winter. She has had a very long-lasting illness. She is still not well. She came home 3 weeks ago. She can now begin to walk around a little but it does not look like she will be able to start her school. It starts in the beginning of May. Julia has attended Sine's school all winter. She finishes next Friday. Then she will come home but only for 5 days. Then her school starts again. She is going down to have school for 3 1/2 months.

Gertrude is home now, but this summer she wants to find a job. The boys are all well and work. Herman has been ill most of the winter, but he is now much better.

It has been a hard time for us, we had only a little to sell and it did not bring in much, but we did not suffer any want. It would have helped if Sine had not gotten sick. But yet we do not know what is best for us. I thank the Lord that He let her live and I hope that her illness will stand her in good stead so she will learn to seek the right doctor. As Christians we all have to seek God both in prosperity and adversity.

Oh, how I long to talk to you. So often I think that if I could only come to a Danish church and hear a good sermon or if I could only meet some true children of God, but that is of course impossible for me. Pray for me, dear Christian, and for all of us that we in our faith will cling to our dear Savior.

Have you heard from Denmark lately? I got a letter from my sister Sidsel Marie not long ago. She wrote that your mother has been ill for a while but now she is much better. She also wrote that my sister Maren is still lying the same way. It must have been hard for her.

Has Otto gone home yet?

We wish you every success with your beloved. I hope you can come out and visit us some day. Greet your brothers from us. The dearest greetings from all of us but first and last from me.

 Your aunt,

Johanne Nielsen

Write as soon as you can. I long to hear whether you received our letters.

The Railroads

*Most immigrants arriving in the United States during the last decades of the
nineteenth century were able to travel by rail if not directly to their final destination
at least very close to it. Such was the case with Herman and Johanne Nielsen who
arrived in Algona, Iowa by train.*

*Railroading was attaining the golden age of its existence. These were the years of
nearly unbridled expansion when railroad stocks soared and lines were extended to
remote villages transforming them into bustling communities. Transportation of
freight increased significantly with farmers receiving higher prices for produce sold
at rail terminals than at other locations. However, when there was collusion among
railroads farmers felt themselves victimized. At the same time, however, passenger
travel was often tedious and slow on the branch lines where the trains stopped to load
and unload freight. Even on main lines passenger travel was delayed because
competing railroads were reluctant to synchronize schedules and travellers often had
to switch lines and stations taking what were very indirect routes to their destina-
tions.*

*Algona, a town of 2,911 population in 1900, had three railroads serving it, each
with its separate depot. They were the Chicago-Northwestern, the Iowa Central (later
the Minneapolis and St. Louis), and the Milwaukee Road. Most of these trains
burned Iowa coal, high in sulphur and cinders. They might reach 25 miles an hour
on a good straightaway, but usually they were slower taking about an hour for the
twelve mile trip from Algona to Luverne with stops at Irvington and Galbraith.*

*Because Pullman or sleeper cars were not always available for long distance journeys,
passengers frequently only travelled by day, stopping at night at hotels that custom-
arily were situated near the depots.*

*Depots in the small towns invariably consisted of a large waiting room with straight,
wooden, high-backed benches, arranged around a cast iron stove located in either the
center or at one end of the room. Spitoons were abundant. A blackboard containing
the chalked schedules was mounted on the wall near the window behind which the
agent wearing a green-visored cap sold tickets and offered information. The sporadic
click of the telegraph receiver was conspicuous. Outside the waiting room was a
board platform from which passengers could board or depart the trains. If the
community was fortunate, this platform was of brick.*

*Most railroad lines offered pastors, priests, and other full-time religious personnel
special consideration. Sometimes this was in the form of free passes, more often in
greatly reduced fares or coupons. Instances of most of these practices are found in the
letters.*

Carol may have recovered from her prolonged bout with typhoid fever but then Herman became seriously ill necessitating the daughters being summoned home from Washington. Marie arrives after a most gruelling journey by train; Laurine who is not well, probably due to another pregnancy, does not come home.

Algona, Iowa
July 6, 1894

Dear Chrestian (Christian),

It has not been long since we received a card from you, and I should have written long ago but I waited to write until I saw how Herman was doing. He got very ill. Right after you left we had the doctor out here 7 times, and one of the times two doctors were here. They gave him the latest medicine they knew of, and they said that if the blood would not stop, he could not live for more than two days. It is a vein that has a hole. He was so ill he could not either talk or move, but after he had laid still for a week, it stopped. We got Julia and Sine (Carol) home from their schools, and we telegraphed for them in Washington. Marie came home, but Laurine could not come; she is not well. Marie had the most difficult journey she has ever had. She travelled for 9 days but by the help of God she came home to us again. Herman was much better when she came home. Now he can walk around, but he cannot do anything.

Oh, dear Christian, you cannot imagine how glad I was when Herman was very ill, he asked all of us to pray with him. And he asked me to read about the prodigal son for him. As he came to his Father, so shall we come to our Father if we would be blessed, and that was exactly the word I wanted so much to hear, because if we do not turn to him and ask for help, then we cannot be helped. And he urgently asked us to seek our Savior and pray with each other so that some day we could all gather in the Kingdom of God. Oh, I have so much to thank our Lord for. He has heard my prayer and I will ask him to help us hereafter to live a Christlike life whether it is for better or worse.

How are you up there? Are there any children of God there? Are you lonely? We long to hear from you.

Now I will let you know how we are. It looks like we will get the best crop that we have ever had, but we do not have much land besides our own. Marie is glad that she came home to see us. Now she does not want to leave until her doctor asks for her. Julia is now back at her school. She has still one week left. Gertrude is home and goes to school, and Sine (Carol) is also home now for a short time. Have you written home to Denmark or have you heard from there recently? Marie asked me to greet you from herself and from Laurine. Laurine is fine, and I learned from Marie that she holds on to our Lord which makes me most happy.

Now best regards to you from all of us.
Live well in the Lord.

From your aunt,

Johanne Nielsen

Marie has remained in Algona for the summer and fall but is now intimating that she will return to Washington. It is not indicated whether or not her doctor friend has urged her to do so. Laurine has had her fourth child, another son. Carol and Julia are continuing to teach school, and Gertrude is studying to be a teacher. The letter makes reference to the devastating tornado that swept through Kossuth County in 1894.

Algona, Iowa
October 24, 1894

Dear Chrestian (Christian),

I will write you a few words because I know that you would like to hear from us. I waited till <u>Hyrderøsten</u> came because I was hoping that your address would be in it, but it was not, so I will write you at the address you sent me in your last letter. I thank you very much for your letter. I read your letters several times, and I felt like I was actually talking to you. Oh, I wish you were here now that Marie is home. Marie is a godfearing girl and so is Laurine according to Marie.

I have, as you so often have said, much to thank our Lord for. Herman is now as well as he was before, and the rest of us are all well. Marie is probably going back to Washington; she misses them.

Now Laurine has four small children, 3 boys and a girl. She is doing fine, but she longs to come home. Sine(Carol) and Julia are now both second year teachers and Gertrude now goes to normal school.

You have probably heard about the cyclone which has been here. It was 3 miles north of us, and it did cause great damage. We have reason to thank and praise God for saving us. You wrote and asked about the photographs, but they do not have any left. If they get some again, I will remember you.

Write soon, and let us know how you all are. Greet your brothers from us. Marie asked me to greet you from her, and now the dearest greetings from all of us.

From your aunt,

Johanne Nielsen

Sorry about my short letter.

HAN 988 3-1-21 Danish

Christian Mengers and Dorthea Henriksen at the time of their marriage in 1895.

44

In this letter, which is a copy of one that Christian sent to his sister Ane and her husband Hans Weimar in Denmark, he describes his marriage to Dorthea. Although there is no mention of it, he was ordained into the Lutheran ministry on May 20, 1894, after attending P.C. Trandberg's theological seminary in Chicago. The letter becomes a short sermon. Henrik , who is referred to, is Ane and Weimar's eldest son.

Box 694
Dwight, Illinois
May 8, 1895

Dear brother-in-law (Hans Weimar) and sister (Ane) with children,

May God's peace be with you, Ane. You asked me to write again soon, but that did not happen because many things have taken my time. Changing travel plans: I have had a rich experience in good and bad fortune, along with the hundreds of things which have filled my mind and thoughts, and when I do not have some peace of mind I do not write letters that are not highly necessary.

Since I got your letter I have been in Chicago 1/2 a year and where I am now I have stayed for a couple of months.

Now Dora and I are married. Our wedding was March first and shortly afterwards we travelled to a city 75 miles from Chicago.

The wedding was a beautiful and delightful festivity, a day that was the best I had ever seen, and since then I have had only delightful days. Brightness and joy have filled our home, which is always neat and in good order. Our joy has its origin in Jesus, the Savior, our heavenly bridegroom. With him we unite in prayer every day. Earthly riches is not our fortune - even if we had some it would not bring good fortune that could be a foundation - no, but the heavenly is our riches, and that is our fortune, and we are united in this and we love our common Savior, and we have understood that only in that is life what it should be.

Dear Ane, it is such a long time since I wrote to our dear parents, so I will make this letter short and write to them. How are you, are you all well?

Dear Weimar, I long to see and talk to both you and my sister Ane; how are things going in your business, is it progressing? Yes, if there is progress in spiritual matters, if you are thinking at all about heaven do not bind your thoughts too much to the earth and all that belongs to it and toward life on earth, for this word of God says, "The world will pass away, and the delights thereof but whoever does God's will will endure to eternal life. Heaven and earth will pass away but not a jot or a letter of the law shall pass away until it all ends." We belong to the eternal, our life here will soon disappear and then the eternal life begins either in shocking horror or glorious joy. And what happens after death depends on how we used the time of grace here, if we thought that we were lost sinners who must early and late depend on Jesus for cleansing and forgiveness of sins after we have first become his children through faith in his blood - and sacrifice for us.

Henrik writes that he goes to Sunday School. I am happy for this, let him and all your children go regularly, when it is possible, but dear sister and brother, do not neglect that you yourselves attend Christian meetings and worship services, because it is more important than for your children, because if they should die as children they would be saved; but adults will not be saved if they have not become God's children by means of faith, and faith comes by hearing, and hearing comes from God's word, and therefore it is necessary to hear God's word in order to come to faith which is a solid conviction that one is a child of God and heir to life.

Yes, Henrik is a fine boy. He writes wisely and well, and that was a good letter for a boy of his age. Let him write again, now this time I cannot write anything to him, but next time he will get a letter from Uncle Christian.

Loving greetings to both of you, Ane and Vejmar(Weimar) and your boys.

From your brother and sister,

Dora and Christian.

Address: Rev. Chr. C. Mengers
Box 694 Dwight, Ill.
North America

Very likely this is the picture that Julia Nielsen gave her students and that
Tante Johanne sent to Christian.

Following his ordination Christian has begun serving a Danish congregation in Dwight, Illinois. Christian's brother Valdemar with Laura and Leah have returned to Denmark, and Johanne's sister Maren has died after her prolonged suffering. Mrs. Heede is the wife of an early Danish pastor and friend of Christian. The letter indicates that the Nielsen daughters are teaching and the sons are harvesting three farms besides their own.

Algona, Iowa
July 21, 1895

Dear Chestian (Christian),

It has now already been a long time since we received your highly welcomed letter, and I thank you so much. There is no point in my apologizing for not writing you sooner. The reason for it is that I have a hard time collecting my thoughts, but I long to hear from you. Therefore I must hurry up and write because I know you are a slow writer just like I am!

I long for your letters, and even more I long to talk to you. Oh, how I would love to hear you preach, but of course that is impossible. I hope that with God's help you will do fine up there in Dwight. I think it is a difficult position up there, not many can bear to hear the truth. May the good God open their eyes so the Word can enter their hearts and work the salvation of their souls.

Now I will let you know how we all are. We are all well. Herman has been much better this summer than he was last summer. All the girls are home at the moment. Sine (Carol) is teaching our home school this summer and also in the winter. Julia's school starts in a month. Gertrude has a school 6 miles from here for the winter. We had a good crop this year. Christian and Niels go out every day with harvest machinery and 5 horses, for they shall harvest three other farms besides our own.

Have you heard from Denmark lately? How are they at home? I have not heard since Valdemar wrote that my sister Maren had died. Are they more satisfied to live in Denmark than here? I would like to know how things are at home. I long to come home to Denmark once again and see my sisters, and the girls have promised to help me. Maybe next summer if it is God's will. They all say I will regret it if I take such a trip, but I will just leave it in God's hands and his will.

I read in <u>Hyrderøsten</u> that Mrs. Heede died. That will be a great sorrow for him, but what a joy when such a godly soul goes home, for I am sure that is what she was.

We have not had any photographs, except one of Julia she took to give to her children the last day of school. I will send you one, for I think it is better than the last little one you have.

Loving greetings to you and your wife from us all, but first and last from me.

Your aunt,

Johanne Nielsen

Let us know how Viggo is. Greet him from us all.

This short note indicates that Christian is planning a visit to Algona. There is no indication that Dorthea will accompany him. Wives so often had to remain at home. The fellowship of other Danes who were expressive of their faith was highly cherished by Johanne and Christian. Johanne's children who were thoroughly Americanized may not have placed the same value on such associations.

Algona, Iowa
September 4, 1895

Dear cousin Christ,

We received your letter. We are very glad that you are coming to see us, but we hope that you can manage to get here before Julia and I go away to our schools. We go September 14th.

You heard Rev. Engholm was here a short time ago. Mamma invited him down to spend a few days when you come, therefore you will not be alone while you are here. We have found some good Christian Danish people whom you will appreciate. I should like to go with you to see them, if you could only manage to get here before the 14th. Carl is waiting to take my letter to town therefore, goodbye for this time.

Your cousin,

Carol

P.S. Mamma received Viggo's letter and will answer as soon as she can.

Although the Nielsens' material state has improved with a new house that the girls (Carol, Julia and Gertrude) have had built for them, Johanne continues to long for correspondence and spiritual inspiration, and Herman's health continues to be precarious. Carol is following her sisters to Washington where Marie has married her doctor and Laurine has had another child. Johanne longs to accompany Christian and Viggo on their planned trip to Denmark and believes that the girls might be able to provide the money. Louis and his family referred to at the conclusion of the letter was a mutual acquaintance from Streator, Illinois.

Algona, Iowa
April 12, 1896

Dear Chrestian (Christian),

Today I will write you a few words. I long to hear how both of you are doing and if you are both well. You wrote, dear Christian, that you would write before you came out here. I have waited so long for a letter from you but in vain. You know that your letters always are a comfort and encouragement for me, but I also know that you have many to write to and you are probably very busy too.

Now I will let you know how we all are. We are all well except for Herman. He is not well, but he is better now than he has been. The three girls all tend schools around here. They have now built us a new house. Now we wish that you could come out and visit us and stay here for a while. We have more room now, and how wonderful it would be to hear one of you, you or Viggo, preach. When you write to him, please greet him from us and thank him for the letter that he wrote us, and tell him that he can come out here in his free time if he wants to. We can find a place where he can hold meetings.

Our girls will stay around here for the summer, but in July, when Carol is done with her school, she is probably going to Washington. Marie has been married to the doctor, who we talked about when you were here. She now lives quite a way from where Laurine lives. They are all well. Laurine now has five small children. She writes that they will all come home in two years if it is God's will.

You wrote in a letter to us that you thought of going to Denmark when Viggo is done studying. Oh, that would make me so happy if that could happen, but God alone knows. I would love to accompany you.

I think that the girls could get the money for my journey, but I doubt that I will have the courage to travel alone. I will leave it in God's hands. Let me know when you write what you think about it.

Have you heard from Louises in Streator? They wrote from Washington that they had heard that he was sick. Now, dearest greetings from all of us to you and your wife and first and last from me.

Your aunt,

Johanne Nielsen.

This letter to Christian, who is now a pastor in Philadelphia, from his brother Viggo reveals a lighter side of life in the Nielsen household and some interesting insights into his various cousins. As one studying for the ministry, Viggo exhibits both a deliberate religious concern and a playful spirit. Denominational prejudices, characteristic of the day, are very evident. References to a number of Danish Lutheran pastors and preaching places appear as does a reference to Gothuldine Trandberg, the widow of P.C. Trandberg, the theological professor who had died earlier in the summer. Viggo's travels are possible because of the railroad pass that he possesses.

Box 193
Algona, Iowa
August 12, 1896

Dear Christian and Dora,

Yes, I am still in Iowa and very comfortable here at uncles. You (singular) know - sorry, I nearly forgot to include my beloved sister-in-law. You (plural) know that when I left Heedes I went to Graettinger where I started July 4 and 5 by preaching Saturday forenoon. Sunday noon a group picture was taken in front of the church. Bing, Heede, Simonsen from Spencer, Dixen, Engholm, and I all were present and preached, Otto Sorensen whom you probably know has decided to go to Africa in a few years. First he must study 1 year in college and 1 year at some missionary school. All who know you send greetings.

From Graettinger I came here to Algona a week or so before Carol left for Washington. She is in my opinion a lovely girl. In fact I think our cousins have changed a lot since you were here. I am just sorry I did not have a chance to talk more to Carol. Just before she left, Carol, Julia, Gerty (Gertrude), Christian, Niels and I were in Algona and had our pictures taken.

When I had been here about a week, Engholm and Heede dropped in on their way to Bing in Britt. They were here from 9 a.m. till 6 p.m. From Britt they went to Minneapolis to help Mrs. Trandberg move. As far as I know she is now enroute to Denmark. The Sunday Engholm and Heede were in Britt, I preached in Graettinger. Last Sunday I preached in the Congregational Church in Wesley, where Andreasen from St. Paul will preach at the end of the month. I would like to talk to him but it will not be this time. I had promised to be back in Chicago by this time, but I have no money to travel, and when I do get there I will have hundreds of things to take care of. They

Top: The young theological student, Viggo Mengers, at the time that he
visited Tante Johanne and her family.

Bottom: Viggo Mengers writes of swimming with his cousins at night in the
West Des Moines River that flows through Algona.

54

will give me gray hair.

Tante, Julia and Gerty drove to Wesley in J and G's buggy pulled by two beautiful little ponies. I rode on Topsy. There is a lot to tell about but it will be easier to tell than write if we see each other again. Nearly every day I drive to town with my cousins' buggy and ponies, and then we ride horse and saddle on the prairie worse than any cowboy. Christian bought a fine saddle one day and Julia has a fine riding whip. I wish I had them in Chicago. If I ever have lived a fairy tale, this is it. One night Christian, Niels, Carol and I went swimming in the Des Moines River. Niels rode, we three rode in the buggy. Chris jumped in and cut his foot on a piece of barbed wire in the water. Then I tore my foot on a nail or something in a boat we were using. It was so dark I thought it was mud I was washing off, till I discovered it was blood streaming out. And while I stood there washing off my foot we heard a couple of wolves howling. Lightning quick we gathered our stuff together and with great difficulty got over a wire fence, jumped in the wagon with Niels on the horse and beat the horses until we were stuck in the middle of the forest that lies along the river. We had lost our way. Half dressed we ran around, bumping into trees instead of avoiding them, blood streaming from the feet and a pair of wolves howling behind us, a hill with tall trees before us, no road to be seen in the utter darkness. The wolves had evidently heard us splashing at the swimming hole. It was all exciting. Niels tore around like an Indian to find a way out but did not find any. A fine situation! Chris jumped off the wagon and yelled at the top of his voice for 15 minutes. Finally a man came. He had been County Superintendent and lighted us out of the darkness with a lantern. After some difficulty we got out of the thicket and onto a road, but the wolves had been probably thirty steps away from us before the light shone. Probably the light and the screaming scared them off. I lost my tuning fork in the commotion. When we got home about midnight we bandaged our feet. Chris was no worse than he could work the next day, though with pain, but I was an invalid for a couple of days.

Now we have survived the scratches and the fright. By the way, Julia is the sweetest of them all - except for one thing - she is my cousin. You can imagine the rest . We have been riding together a couple of times, she on Dolly and I on Topsy. She has a fine ladies' riding saddle. I have become an expert in horsemanship, so if it were not for the fact that I am studying theology, I would surely become a cowboy on the western prairies. Julia and I usually go riding together. Yesterday we were in Algona and I took her for a ride. She and Gerty were in there for a 2 week institute which is over on Saturday. Tonight I will go in to mail this letter and take Gerty for a ride so she will not feel neglected . For each time I take her along, I usually take Julia a couple of times, because we get along best. We all get along well, but Miss Gerty has a little streak of stubborness, but I think she has a firm character. I really love all my cousins here but especially J.

I have had a job converting my family from the Reformed faith to the Lutheran, and I think I have partly succeeded. The Reformed faith is water compared to the Lutheran, so superficial, insignificant, and confusing, that it makes me sick to think about it. The Episcopal church here is dry formalism. The Methodists are blindly zealous, full of errors, though I feel they have done a reforming work here. As far as I can see the Congregational church is play acting and illusion.

One thing I love about all our cousins, they are wise and sensible but they do not think more of themselves than they ought. Rather they think less of themselves than they have reason to, and they are willing to listen in the realm of Christianity in spite of the poor religious environment here. There was a revivalist preacher here a year or so ago who opened their eyes to the sinfulness of playing cards, dancing, etc. He influenced them to read the Bible and pray in the evening, and yet they did not know what Christianity is all about - the fruit of the reformed churches. They do not consider themselves Christians, though, they pray, read the Bible, and try to be as good as they can wherever they are. This is true because on the way from Algona to Uncle's I heard about their good children. (It happened I did not take the train I had planned on to Algona, and Julia came too late, so I rode with someone who did not know them except that "the school ma'ams are real good girls.")

There was a slavery to the reformed works-righteousness, so that their souls were not freed through Christ. I have often spoken to them about what I and our church understand by true and biblical Christianity. One day when we had visited the 3 sisters, all teachers, Gertie spoke up on the way home after we had spoken about these things: " Now I understand what Christianity is. I did never understand it before." We had talked about these things on a trip by buggy and ponies to Minnesota where she will teach this fall, about a mile from the Minn. border. We were at Elmore, Minn.

The first of the week I plan to go to Chicago if I can get the money. I have written Garmoe to ask him to lend me $5.00 but have not had an answer. Julia asked me last night if I needed money, and if I did, she would help. I have not let on that I am short, and I do not want to borrow from uncles, if I can help it.

I am glad things have gone well for you up to now and I hope for your success there. And I am glad Rev. Schaeffer was present. Do you have a robe? I think I will see Nielsen in Chicago if all goes well. There are lots of things I would like to talk to you about, especially about this Iowa trip, but it won't be now. I have a joint permit for 39 railroad lines until Sept. 30, 1896.

Christian, I will give you good advice. Study your sermons well and if you can, get Weidner's Studies in the Book. These books have had real value for me. It may seem dry at first but has outlines and sketches for thousands of sermons, and is true Lutheran stuff. I have learned to prize it greatly.

Is this letter long enough? Write soon! With greetings to you both from Aunt, Uncle, cousins and me, I send you wishes for the Lord's blessing to your body and soul where you are.

Your brother,

Viggo

Do not forget to write. Tante would like your photographs. Write right away. It takes less than two days. The last one left Philadelphia. Aug. 4, 7:30 p.m. and was in Algona Aug. 6 at 5 p.m. So both of you write a long letter right now whether you have time or not. "Bellarina" [sic.] will not disturb you.

Julia Nielsen mentions "the merry chimes of sleigh bells" in a letter to her cousin Christian.

Julia has transcribed a hymn for Christian which is the occasion of this letter. It also refers to teaching and family health. Another mode of travel occurs with the reference to "the merry chime of the sleigh bells."

Algona, Iowa
December 19, 1896

Mr. C. C. Mengers
Philadelphia, Pennsylvania

Dear cousin Christ,

I will now fulfill the promise I made you five or six years ago in regard to the song "Sitting at the feet of Jesus." I will send it with this mail. I do not know whether you can read it or not, but it is the best that I can do. You know I am no musician, and therefore know nothing about music.

Gertrude and I are both teaching again, and we are both boarding at home. Gertrude is teaching five miles from home and drives the ponies. I am teaching the home school. All the children go to school. I have a very nice school. I am glad that I am not teaching the Sexton school again.

So far we have had a beautiful winter. There is just snow enough for a sleigh now and then. I love to hear the merry chime of the sleigh bells. Papa, mamma and all of us are well and prospering. Today is a beautiful sunny day. I must go to town. So I do not have time to write any more. Hoping you are well and happy, I will close my little note for this time. With our best regards to you and your wife. Goodbye,

Your cousin,

Julia Nielsen

P.S. Mamma tells me to tell you she is waiting patiently for your pictures.

This letter thanks Christian for the picture he has sent and mentions the birth of Agatha, Christian and Dorthea's daughter. After family news, she again refers to the longed for trip to Denmark.

Algona, Iowa
January 28, 1897

Dear Chrestian (Christian),

I will try to write a little letter to you. First I must ask you to excuse me for waiting so long to write. I have begun several times but have not finished any. It seems I cannot gather my thoughts unless I am alone, and then there is so much to do.

First, I will thank you so much for the picture. It is very good and an excellent likeness. We all send congratulations on the birth of your little girl and hope you are all well.

We are all well, and all are in school. There is no one home except Herman and me. Gertrude boards at home and drives five miles to and from school every day. We have not had a very cold winter until now, but this is the coldest it has been for many years.

We just had a letter from the three in Washington. They are all well. Sine (Carol) writes that she doubts Laurine will be home this summer. She does not see how she can travel with so many children. I think Laurine lives in hope of getting home. Poor Rine, she wishes so much to be here. She is like me. We had a letter from Viggo at Christmas and he mentioned that you planned on a trip to Denmark. I do not know when, but if you are thinking of this summer, would you write before too long and I will see if I cannot arrange to go along? I doubt I will ever be brave enough to travel alone.

Now I will finish my writing for the time is 12 midnight. I must get to bed.

Live well, dear friends, till we see you. Hearty greetings from us all, but first and most from me.

Your aunt,

Johanne Nielsen

HAN 988 53-3-36 Danish

The Spanish American War

The first era of American confrontational expansion had occurred over a half century earlier driven and sustained by such popular slogans as "54-40 or Fight" and "Remember the Alamo." The result was the acquisition of Oregon, the Mexican War and the eventual annexation of the entire Southwest from Texas to California. Americans seemed to have viewed the events as the inevitable consequences of a "manifest destiny" for them and their nation. Most other countries, though not as enthusiastic, were not hostile.

When the United States launched a second period of confrontational expansion in the late 1890's against a seriously weakened Spain, the response was rather different. The slogan "Remember the Maine" had to be vigorously undergirded both in the United States and throughout the world by a constant barrage of journalistic and political propaganda ranging from descriptions of morally depraved Spaniards to a President receiving God's endorsement for war. "Manifest destiny" was difficult to apply to Cuba, Puerto Rico and the Philippines, and even today questions remain concerning the events that triggered the conflict. Most Americans supported their country. Foreign governments and their peoples, however, were less accepting of the American explanations and actions. This may have been due partly because other small colonial countries such as Portugal, the Netherlands, Belgium and Denmark saw themselves as potential victims of larger powers. Furthermore, the great powers could not help but detect the emergence of a potential rival: politically, militarily, and most certainly economically. The European public response was undoubtedly partly due to a population that had become better educated and informed and that held ever increasing liberal and democratic views. Such are the elements that one detects in the letters of Niels Christiansen from Denmark to his brother, C.C. Mengers, in the United States.

A grouping of members of the Christiansen family taken in Denmark. Three of them write letters in this book; all are mentioned. They are left to right: Niels, Paul and Juliane Christiansen, Dora and Viggo Mengers, and Caroline Christiansen.

62

Niels, Christian's elder brother who is a teacher, writes letters that contain much more than family news, although this letter does report that Johanne has finally realized her dream of visiting Denmark and that Valdemar and his family have returned to live there. The letter also reveals Christian's interest in the Danish philosopher and religious thinker, Søren Kierkegaard, and in Bishop H. Martensen, the ethicist and theologian, as well as the popular novelist, Carit Etlar. Niels' views on the Spanish-American War provide insight into how Europeans assessed this conflict between the United States and Spain. Multe, who is referred to at the end of the letter, is Niels' wife, Juliane, and Paul is their son.

Amakke paa Holbæk, Denmark
August 1, 1898

Dear brother and sister-in-law (Christian and Dora),

Finally I start a letter to you, not without shame. I cannot even say how long it is since I wrote, and I can imagine, dear brother, that you in a foreign land sometimes, or always, feel abandoned more than we others whom you left, because we live in our usual surroundings which you also have had to separate yourselves from. I think I must require more of myself regarding correspondence than I can expect of you or Viggo. So I must improve my letter writing, but I will not promise because broken promises are a heavy load on the back.

I can give you only sparse information about books. The used bookstore does not know the prices of Kierkegaard's works and, in any case, you probably can get only single volumes, not sets. If I had remembered before I left on vacation, I could have asked in a bookstore. When I get home I will make every effort to do so. Carit Etlar's pamphlets in collection cost about 100 kroner. Maybe I can get an estimate of his best books in hardback. Martensen's <u>Dogmatics</u> 10 1/2 kroner, used, 7 kroner. <u>The Christian Ethic</u> 28 kroner, used, 18 kroner.

Valdemar has the hymnbook you sent, and I suppose you have heard from him by now. If not, I will send the address. Helges Vej 6, 4th Floor, Copenhagen K.

Thank you for your good wishes for my birthday and Valdemar's. Now yours is coming on the 19th and I have promised myself that you will not be without Multe's and my good wishes for your 35th birthday. We hope the Lord will allow you a glad and blessed day for you and yours, and that he will let your new year be bright and good in every way. I have read Ps. 103. It is good when we from a full and warm heart can make those words our own.

I do not have your letter with me unfortunately, so I may have forgotten something of it. Also I left your address at home, so I will send this letter to Caroline in Copenhagen so she can address it. Tante Johanne is in Denmark so I will no doubt be seeing her. It is 25-30 years since I saw her last.

I am looking forward to seeing both you and Viggo. Cannot you afford to come with him in 1900 since he expects to come here and go to Paris too? Do you still have only little Agatha? Is she well and growing tall and strong? Are you and your wife doing well? Do not punish me, but write soon again. I will write to Viggo soon. I can send it to Blair, can I not? Even if he is not there after June 1, I suppose he will still get it. If he should visit you give him my greetings. He wrote to me that he was planning to travel this summer; But do tell me for once, you mysterious new Americans, how is it that earlier you and now Viggo can travel about all of North America? One would think you travel free, explain it to me!

When you get this letter, the disgusting war you are conducting against Spain will hopefully be over. It is not likely that your view and mine agree. I am not interested in Spanish control and I know it is bad, but that does not justify America's presence in Cuba. Who has for the last three years brought on the impossible situation that brought on the war? Is it not American money that has kept the insurgents going and caused both Spanish and Cuban deaths and misery? Is not most of the bad situation in Cuba when the war began caused by American moneymen and their raw and brutal acts? And was the declaration of war necessary? Absolutely not! America could by threats have created bearable and good times for Cuba without costing a single life. One gets the feeling that a little easy war where one of course must be the victor would be quite interesting, especially when Cuba could be freed from the yoke and for no gain to the winner, and for only humanitarian reasons. There is not even a whiff of selfishness nor war-lust. Maybe even Christian love and the Lord Himself drove the noble people to war? As the Jesuits say, the end justifies the means, even if that causes death, sorrow, physical pain and suffering for thousands. And reading the bombastic victory telegrams from Washington makes one wonder whether to laugh or cry. The old Danish understanding is that a victory worth talking about is after a war between two equal adversaries or perhaps even against a stronger one, driven by enthusiasm for saving one's country which leads to personal courage, endurance and bravery. When a colossus tips and is crushed, we call it an accident. When a living colossus decides to crush, we call it a crime. What is America but a money colossus? America's victories in this case leave a bad taste in the mouth. And the way the press agitates, blinds even sensible and enlightened men. I was surprised to see that 58 pastors had signed a letter of commendation to the president expressing their sympathy with the

64

government's attitude to Spain. Are they afraid of not being considered loyal citizens if they had been quiet, or do they actually approve of the murderous war? The good preachers can hardly pray seriously "deliver us from evil" when they agree with a war in which one can hardly find any good thing. What good there is could have been achieved in a more humane way. This is my private opinion about the war, and it would interest me to hear your reaction. If you have good grounds for another belief, I have nothing against it.

We are in the country for our usual 2 to 3 weeks of vacation. Paul has whooping cough but will probably get well more quickly in this fresh country air. We others are well and feeling good. Accept our loving greetings to both of you and your little Agatha from Multe, Paul, and your devoted brother and brother-in-law.

Niels

Excuse the fly specks on the paper. I was not careful enough now that the warm days have finally come. We have had an unusually cold summer so far.

(Note from Caroline)

Greet Viggo if he is with you.

Caroline

Caroline Christiansen
Apotheker (druggist) Nyholm
Amicis Vej 2 St. (stuen)
København

Three generations of the Christiansen family, Paul, Anders and Niels. Anders is the father of Niels, Otto, and Valdemar, all mentioned in the letters, and of Christian and Viggo who took the Mengers name when they immigrated to America.

66

This birthday letter to Christian from his father, Anders Christiansen, is a poignant expression of parental concern. It is an account both of personal faith and of the perplexing human question, Why? Reference is also made to Johanne's current visit to Denmark.

Fredericia, Denmark
August 10, 1898

Dear son (Christian),

For your 35th birthday August 19, your mother and I send our heartiest congratulations. We wish you and your family the grace of our Lord Jesus Christ, the love of God the Father and the Holy Spirit's communion. If the Holy Spirit can draw us to the Father and the Son, that is the best happiness we can wish for in this world, and we will not need to worry about what will meet us in this world or the next, and if we lay our sorrows in God's hand, He will give us strength to overcome everything in life or in life and death. Often we feel so powerless against the many enemies we have to fight against both within and without. If we then would hurry into the out-stretched arms of God, we would feel as safe as a baby in mother's arms. Then a blessed peace will fill our hearts and give our lives a quiet and peaceful stamp. May the Lord give us all grace to do so.

There is a little word that so often sneaks in - the little word WHY. The first time I remember it in my life was when, as a barefoot little child, I had to herd the cattle in field and meadow in rain and wind. Why did I have to be born to poor parents and have to have such trouble? Why was I not a prince or a son of a rich man so I could have nice clothes and shoes and not have to work for strangers who were not always good or nice to me? At that time I did not understand it, but soon I realized that my Heavenly Father had planned this for my own good, because He could see that, in the long run, it was the only way I could make it.

When I was older, I dreamed of a happy family life, but sickness and poverty were my lot. There came that WHY again. Why can I not be well? Why can I not earn enough so my family would not be in sorrow and need? Then God's word came: "Everything works for good to those who love God." Then when the children were grown, I hoped they would have a better life than we had had, and we could visit them and enjoy their well-being. Instead they scattered to the four winds and we have not always been happy for all of them. WHY can we not have as much joy of our children as so many other parents have? Did we not know how to bring them up right, or have we not prayed sincerely enough? This is a more difficult WHY than the others, because if we are on by-ways it is not God's fault, it is our own. But we will pray and believe, and it is our conviction that God has many ways and many means by which He can draw people to Himself, and we believe He has the will to do so, since He so loved the world that He did not spare His own Son but sent Him to die in order to save us.

Of late the WHY has come to me so often. Why do we hear from you so seldom? Is it because I write less often than I should? I do not think so. I wrote to Viggo for his birthday and sent photographs but have not heard from him since. We do not know if he got the pictures or not. He last wrote in January. That is a long time to wait for a letter from a child when you daily wonder how he is. And when one looks back on one's life, there are so many things that come up. Why did one do this or that? If one had done differently, maybe we now would be happier, or maybe someone else would be happier if we had not neglected to lift the burden. But we know that God does not give us burdens to bear without also giving the strength to bear them. The Good Shepherd was with us all and will lead us in green pastures and to running waters, to give us the water of everlasting life to drink.

Your Tante Johanne is in Denmark and has been with us for two weeks. Just now she is in the country. Viggo may be with you just now. Greet him and let him write home soon. Loving greetings to you and your wife and daughter from Ane, her husband and children, but especially from us, your mother and me.

A. Christiansen

While Johanne is enjoying in Denmark the fellowship of family and church that she has missed so much for almost thirty years in America, her husband and children on the other side of the ocean are desperate for news about her. Only the daughters in Washington have had a letter since summer. One wonders whether Johanne in order to prolong her stay was intentionally making it difficult for the family to send her return fare. After Gertrude conveys information about her sisters' teaching positions in Washington, she comments upon Viggo's having been in Canada. Then she writes about her brother Christian's visit to Algona from the oil fields and of Niels' farming activities, but no amount of news can disguise her concern for her mother. As the letter concludes, her desperation is almost overwhelming.

Algona, Iowa
October 31, 1898

My dear cousin Christian,

I wrote to Viggo quite awhile ago but have never heard from him since. I am not sure that I have your right address but I thought I would try and see. Have you heard from Denmark lately? We have not heard from mamma for nearly three months and I am nearly worried sick. We have written three letters and received no answers. Will you not please write to me immediately and tell me if you have heard anything of mamma? She has written but once to the girls out west. Papa has written lately again. I have been away to school, and have just come home. I supposed that they had heard from mamma right along. I cannot see what the reason is. We were going to send her the money to come home on, but we haven't got a good address, so we have been waiting for her to write.

Where is cousin Viggo now? The last I heard of him he was in Canada. Kindly tell him if he wishes to ever hear from Algona again, that he must do me the honor to answer my last letter.

Brother Chris was at home this summer. The rates were cut to $15 each way, so he thought he would run home to see us. He had worked at the pumps for 5 or 6 months and that is so close work. Sister Julia is teaching in New Castle and Carol is teaching at Carbonado, where sister May (Marie) lives. My school opens next Monday. I am hurrying the boys up with husking the corn. I want Neal (Niels) to go to school all winter.

If mamma gets home this winter, I will leave for Washington early enough in the spring for the spring examination. I do hope that she will soon come home. If you have not heard anything of her, will you not write as quickly as possible to Denmark to your papa and ask him to write to us the reason mamma does not write. And please write as soon as you get this whether you have any news of mamma or not.

I am ever,
Your cousin,

Gertrude

All our best regards to your wife.

P. S. I will be almost wild until I hear from you. I have thought of sending a telegram to mamma but it is so very expensive.

Caroline Christiansen was Christian's younger sister and the writer of one of the letters in this book. Tante Johanne thought highly of her.

Danish Christmas preparations play an important part in this letter from Christian's younger sister Caroline who is helping make things for Leah and Ruth (Valdemar and Laura's daughters) and for Ane and Hans Weimar's children. She also indicates that Tante Johanne may be spending Christmas with them and that Otto and Laurine are expecting their fifth child. The reference in this letter to Johanne's many siblings in Denmark suggests that she perhaps had brothers or other sisters than Ane Marie, Sidsel Marie, and Karen Marie.

Copenhagen, Denmark
December 14, 1898

Dear brother and sister-in-law (Christian and Dora),

It is so long since I wrote that I have forgotten when it was, but I do hope I remembered my brother's birthday. This letter is to wish you a very happy Christmas. I suppose you have a tree - most people do, especially when there are children. Last night I was out at Niels'. Multe was so busy sewing doll clothes for Leah and Ruth, so I helped a little. I need to make some decorations to hang on the Christmas tree for Ane's children. There are quite a few, and many are needed to have plenty for all.

I think you know that Tante Hanne (Johanne) is here in Denmark. She and mother were here in Copenhagen for 8 days in October, and we expect Tante Hanne for Christmas though we are not sure about it. She has many siblings that could use her time. She will see you too on her return trip. It would have been nice if she could have visited you first so we could have known how you live. It is more fun to hear it from someone who comes from there.

How is Agatha? Is she 2 or 3? Could we be fortunate enough to receive her picture? We would love to see what a sweet girl she is.

My writing is not on the lines, but I am writing in half darkness, so you will have to excuse it.

Valdemar has moved to:

> Nørrefarimagsgade 37A 1 Sal
> København K

You know that Otto has become a house owner. I have not seen it but I think it is near cooper Nissen's. I think he has it on very easy terms, for you can understand he does not have much money. It is a good thing that he has something that interests him. I think they expect the 5th child before long, a nice little flock.

We are well here, and I hope you are the same.

Now I hope you will have a very happy Christmas and a good New Year.

Loving greetings to you all from your sister-in-law and sister,

Caroline

A garden group of the Christiansen family during Johanne's visit to Denmark. Christian's mother, Ane Marie, is on the extreme left; Tante Johanne is seated to the right of the central pillar.

74

This note from Niels assures Christian of Johanne's pending departure from Denmark. She will follow a customary route crossing the North Sea from Esbjerg to Harwich, then travelling across England by rail to Southampton, and sailing from that port to New York on the St. Paul. From New York Johanne will travel by rail to Philadelphia to visit Christian, Dorthea, and their children.

Copenhagen, Denmark
January 15, 1899

Dear brother and sister-in-law (Christian and Dora),

Tante Johanne is here with us until Wednesday, the 18th. In the morning she will travel via Fredericia and Esbjerg to Harwich and then to Southampton. The emigration steamer "St. Paul" leaves Saturday, the 21st to New York. Then she takes the train to Philadelphia. I wish I could tell you which train, but right now I do not know that, and I am not sure if I can get the information at our emigration office. When I tell you that "St. Paul" leaves Southampton on the 21st, you can perhaps find out when it reaches New York, because it would be good if you could meet Tante at the railroad station. But, in any case, she is preparing herself to use the address to find you.

This is short because I am busy. I am to take Tante out this afternoon.

Thank you for your New Year's letter that I will answer through Tante.

Loving greetings from us for now.

Your devoted brother,

Niels

In this follow-up letter Niels reveals that they have followed the common practice of using the return of a visitor as an opportunity for sending gifts to family in America, this time to Juliane's brother Louis and to Christian and Dorthea. Christian's gift of a Danish dictionary and grammar offers an occasion for a discourse on Danish spelling. Twice in the letter Niels refers to the birth of Christian and Dorthea's son, Ethan. His report on Valdemar's position provides an insight into Danish labor disputes that were rife at the turn of the century, and Christian's dream of home-steading, which eventually he did attempt, evokes friendly ridicule even as he launches a description of Danish community gardens that were established and continue to flourish. Both of these movements were expressions of the social ferment that resulted in the Labor Party heading the government of Denmark in 1902. As in an earlier letter Niels is scathing in his criticism of the United States for its involve-ment in the Spanish-American War, but he expresses a willingness to discuss issues even though he does not anticipate agreement on matters concerning politics or religion.

Copenhagen, Denmark
January 23, 1899

Dear brother and sister-in-law (Christian and Dora),

In my last short letter I had time only to write about Tante's trip, and I hope when you get this letter, she is comfortable with you after a good trip. I have not heard how her baggage was sent from Fredericia but I hope it went as it should. I am expecting that you will help Tante carefully wrap the little things she brought for my brother-in-law Louis if she decides to mail it to him from Philadelphia. We wanted to use the opportunity of Tante's trip to send little remembrances to please as many as possible of you. The big photograph is for the housemother, my dear sister-in-law, if she can find a little spot for it in the parlor.

 Saaby's Dictionary is not a criticism of your letter-writing which is good enough for me. I do not look at the words but at the content and so far I have always been happy for that. Whether you care to study the latest Danish grammar book, I do not know, but you will find it interesting. It is a second edition. This will distinguish itself from the first edition by a page at the end of the book with corrections, which you will need to examine. There are also some changes in spelling, especially that one omits the letter "j" after "g" and "k" and before "e", and "æ" and "ø". Before "o" and "a" when the "j" is not sounded it is dropped, where the "j" is silent. But where the "j" is sounded as before "o", the "j" is retained. Instead of "x" one uses "ks", although I use the "x" because it is easier. [Examples of Danish words appear in the letter but are omitted here.]

Hearty congratulations on the birth of your little son. May he bring you joy and blessing and grow strong and big and good.

Now to answer your long letter which came as a dear new year's greeting on January 1, and I will follow generally in the same order as you wrote. You will hear about Valdemar from Tante. He is doing fairly well now, though 100 kroner per month is not much. What worries me more is whether he can keep his job very long, for the whole big wagon factory is run by Valdemar, with the help of the manager and his brother and some women. Valdemar is coachmaker, painter, office manager, attorney and administrator. The factory has for several years been boycotted by the union which was to be paid 1000 kroner by owner Knudsen, so now he cannot get workers. Instead of paying back the 1000 kroner, his business is being ruined and his stubborn attitude costs many thousands of kroner every year. Valdemar hopes the plant can be sold for the same use, and that he can keep and maybe improve his situation with the new owners. His address is: Vald. Christiansen, Nørre Farimagsgade 37A1, Copenhagen K.

I will get you the book catalogs shortly. It would be nice if we could meet in 1900 and travel home together. I suppose you and Viggo will get there, but I am not so sure I will, but I will be satisfied when you get to Copenhagen. Thank you for the explanation of your travel over there. I can understand that, but I wonder at the high cost. We can now get to Fredericia for 3.75, to Esbjerg for 4.50, and to Frederikshavn from here for 6.00 kroner. However, these are longer trips from Copenhagen and are cheaper. Those shorter trips between outlying towns cost about what they did when you were home.

Is not homesteading pretty much just a saga when one strangely strikes out from the civilized world? For you it cannot be of great value, for you are not a farmer and even if you rent the land out, the population will be too scant to be able to pay a pastor. You do not seriously plan to buy land, do you? Yes, if you can hope to stay in a city for many years or forever, it would be nice to have one's own house with a garden where you can sometimes get fresh air at night instead of living in those horrid huge tenement houses with not a bit of garden. I have a little rented garden of 400 square ells. I belong to a group that has as its object to rent land (usually from the city), subdivide it for small gardens and rent them to poor people for 5, 7, 10 or 20 kroner yearly according to size and location. So each space has a little garden house where the mother and children can spend the whole day in the fresh air in the summer, and the husband can come out in the evening, eat his supper, smoke a pipe, read his paper or do a bit of gardening, play with the children, talk with his wife and the neighbors in the adjoining gardens. This is certainly a communal garden. In our Copenhagen Garden Society we have rented land for 900 families, and other societies have almost as many. This greatly improves family life. The father is not at the public house (saloon) and the children are away from bad company on the streets. The plants are a common new interest for the whole family: what is good for them and what is not, and they take pleasure in their vigorous growth and have here a noble enjoyment which before they had not known and this too often has been neglected.

We hope Dora is well after the event, and that the boy and she are well. You are probably not fit to live with for the pride of having a son, a shoot on the family tree. But a little girl to be a flower on the tree is nice too. I wish we could have had a little girl besides Paul.

I agree with you in the first part of your letter. Regarding Cuba in the last part, I agree in part. Cuba's location indicates that it should belong to the United States or that it should be independent, at least after it became able to stand alone. Spain, I am sure, should not own Cuba, but I think the matter could have been handled without war. Also, I doubt that the U. S. is dealing out of love. A land where money so dominates does not usually act altruistically.

It could be said that the Cuba question was a welcome opportunity to increase the Army and especially the Navy appropriations, so they could later colonize and annex as much land as possible in America or Asia. Where does not really matter. I am actually in opposition to the greed of the great nations against the weaker. The U. S. has been greedy for a long time, and, you will see, it will become increasingly brutal. The Cuba thing started so quietly, but then it would be nice to have Puerto Rico and the Philippines if it works. My sympathy for the U. S. stops right there, for one cannot imagine that the U. S. has the aim of freeing all wronged and oppressed countries, no matter by whom. I am afraid that the U. S. is so human that egoism becomes its driving power as it is everywhere. I will admit that my antipathy to the U. S. is against its people. What I see is a large portion of hypocrisy with tasteless pride, and they have nothing to be proud of. These victories that they have won! Well, never mind. If they help Cuba to a good future, they deserve thanks, anyway. Do you suppose I would be more thankful to the U. S. if my 2 brothers, you and Viggo, had died in the Cuban war? I would thank any nation that would be on our side against Germany so that South Jutland could have its rights especially under the present tyranny. For the South Jutlanders are a part of the Danish nation. You could never care that much about Cubans. Yes, I know about the "Maine," even the smallest child knows that story, and I can understand that the U. S. has grounds for revenge. Is there real proof? Could not the cause be human error? An American paper I read a few months ago declared that the real cause of the sinking would not be known until the Spanish leave. However, I do not doubt that they are the culprits.

78

I can admire your enthusiasm for your new land and I do not doubt there are many people with warm hearts for the wronged and suppressed. If the Americans are driven by such noble motives, I will take off my hat for your flag, disregard small faults and thank you for blood shed in a good cause.

We are all well, as Tante will tell you. Our birthdays are: Paul's, Oct. ll, mine, Oct. 27, Multe's Oct. 30. Thank you for birthday wishes and your new year's greeting. Have a good new year. I have nothing against a good discussion with you, also on religious subjects, though I do not share your view nor your confession, but exchange of thought is not useless. Loving greetings to all four of you and to Tante who is probably with you when you get this letter. Greetings to all from all.

Your devoted brother,

Niels

Gertrude's short letter indicates that the family finally had heard about their mother's return to America both from Johanne herself and from Christian. Not only is Herman ill again but the entire area is recovering from an epidemic of influenza that at the time was referred to as "Lagrippe." The letter also refers to the birth of Christian and Dorthea's son, Ethan.

Algona, Iowa
January 29, 1899

My dear cousin Christ,

It is quite awhile since we received your card. I suppose mamma will soon be with you.

She wrote to us that she expected to leave Copenhagen Jan 18. We have been wishing most heartily that mamma were at home. We have all been sick with the Lagrippe (influenza), but are all recovering, except papa who is having one of his sick spells. I am afraid he is going to be very sick. I wish mamma was at home to take care of him. I cannot do very well at it when I have to teach too. I have had to close school for two weeks on account of sickness.

I believe cousin Viggo wrote that there is a new boy in your home. I hope he is happy and doing well. Should like very much to see him and the rest of your family.

Has the Lagrippe been hard on you? I hope not.

And now with many wishes for a happy New Year I remain,

Your loving cousin,

Gertrude Nielsen

HAN 988 53-3-38 English

For some reason following her visit in Philadelphia Johanne addresses all of her letters to Christian and Dorthea as "Dear friends." The single exception is the last letter before her death. This undated letter obviously from the summer of 1899 contains news about several of the children and makes mention of the marriage of Erik Ericksen, her sister's son who lived on the east coast. Johanne is concerned about maintaining contact with the family wishing that Dora (Dorthea) and the children could visit her if they should travel to Hampton, Nebraska, to visit Dora's family.

Algona, Iowa
[Undated, but summer 1899]

Dear unforgettable friends,

It has been a long time since we received your highly welcomed letter. I would not have waited so long to write you back, but Viggo was here and wrote to you so you already know how we all are. We are all well. Christian came home a few days after Viggo had left. I do not think he will stay here that long; he longs to get back but the weather here is not very pleasant, it is too hot for him. And the money we earn here we really have to work hard for. When Christian leaves, Niels will probably go with him, but they are talking about building a stable first. We got a letter from Julia, a couple of days ago. She did not know whether or not she would get the school in Tacoma. Carol and Gertrude are right now at Laurine's. Gertrude thinks that she will get the school in Newcastle. Laurine and the children will soon travel to Seattle. I was really surprised when I learned that Erik was married. I hope they are all well. Would you please greet all of them from us. I would have written to him but I have lost his address. Would you please send it when you write again. I am glad that little Agatha remembers me. Tell her that I will teach her some more. If only Dora and the children could come and stay here for a while if one day they should travel to Nebraska. It would make us very happy.

Greet Viggo if he is still with you, from all of us. Niels got his letter. I told him to write back but he did not. We also got a notice about a package but it has not arrived yet. Now, dearest greeting to all of you from all of us.

You write, dear Christian, that you did not think that I enjoyed my visit with you but you were wrong. I wish I could do it again.

Johanne Nielsen

Write soon.

Erik Eriksen and his wife. Their marriage and this picture are referred to in the letters. He was a nephew of Tante Johanne and a cousin of Christian.

82

Johanne obviously cherishes the memories of her stay with Christian and his family and indicates that she has read in <u>Danskeren</u>, the publication of the United Danish Evangelical Lutheran Church, that he has resigned from his parish in Philadelphia. With the approach of Christmas she nostalgically returns to the one she spent in Denmark the previous year. This letter assures us that the stable or barn referred to in an earlier letter has been built.

Algona, Iowa
December 10, 1899

Dear friends (Christian and Dora),

First of all I must apologize for not answering your letter sooner. I wrote you a letter some days after I had received your letter, but then I could not get it sent in to town. I thank you so much for the photograph that you sent us; it is so beautiful and clear. I wish that you were closer so that I could talk with you once in a while. Little Ethan looks like Agatha. I wonder if she can still remember me?

I was surprised when I read in <u>Danskeren</u> that you had resigned your place. I hope that you will be able to find a good place, wherever it might be. I think it would be better to live in the eastern states rather than in Nebraska where the winter is so hard. But sometimes we are not in control of these things ourselves.

Have you heard from Denmark recently? You will probably write them for Christmas. I know they are waiting to hear from you. If you write, dear Christian, then I will ask you to greet them all, both old and your siblings from us. Now it is almost Christmas time again, but we do not really feel it here. Oh, what a lovely Christmas I had at home last year; I will never forget it. Here everything is so dead. We never hear the Word. It is not so hard on me because I can read in my Danish books, but the children, I feel terrible when I think about how little they know and how unimportant their poor souls' salvation is to them.

Concerning the temporal, we are all well. Christian and Niels have built a big stable. If Christian stays at home, then they will rent another 160 acres of land, but I do not know how it will turn out. Now I enjoy farming more than I used to, because the prices have gone up.

I have received a letter from Erik. He sent us a photo of himself and his wife.

Now Viggo probably will not go to Denmark. Greet him from us many times.

Just recently we received a letter from Washington. Sine (Carol) and Julia will come and visit us this summer. They are starting to feel homesick.

Now I will end with the dearest greeting to all of you from all of us, but first and last from me, your aunt.

Live well until we see you.

[Unsigned but by Johanne Nielsen]

Agathe Mengers is Christian and Dorthea's daughter. Tante Johanne visits them in Philadelphia on her return from Denmark and frequently mentions Agathe in her letters.

Johanne has experienced gratifying spiritual fellowship at evangelistic meetings called mission meetings by Lutherans. Among the speakers was Jens Dixen, a leading Danish-American lay preacher who travelled widely throughout the world delivering stirring sermons. A highlight of the summer was the visit of Laurine, Carl and their eight children from Washington. The letter refers to acquaintances moving to a Danish settlement in Texas. This reference is to Danevang, near El Campo and southwest of Houston near the Gulf coast. The letter also indicates how much Johanne cherishes her visit with Christian and his family in Philadelphia on her return trip from Denmark.

Algona, Iowa
October 20, 1900

Dear friends (Christian and Dora),

I have waited a long time to hear from you, but now I will write even though I wrote last. I wonder how you all are. Does little Agatha still remember me? Dear Christian, you probably do not realize that your letters have always been a comfort to me, yours and your father's. I read and reread them many times. It is as though I am talking to you. Everything is so depressing here. If only we could have a Danish church here, but I suppose that will not be. I will tell you that a month or so ago I was in Verlev with Skov's. It is 6 miles from here. I was there for two blessed days. The pastor from Britt was there and Jens Dixen from Latimer and 3 Swedish pastors. It was such a treat for me to be among God's children. It is hard to think that it is almost impossible to be with them again. Several people promised to write and tell me when they would have meetings. They asked me to stay with them, but it is probably too far away and too expensive to get there.

Larses in Streator sold their place just before the big flood in Texas, and that is where they had decided to go to the Danish settlement there. When I heard of the terrible weather there, I wrote to ask if they really were going there, and they wrote back that they were going there in fourteen days.

Carl and Laurine and Julia have been home this summer with all their children. They have eight. Carl and Laurine were in Illinois, and Julia stayed here to help us with the children. They were here only 3 weeks and one week in Minnesota because Carl could not be away from his work any longer. Julia promised that they would come this summer because this trip did not cost Julia anything. Julia has a school in Franklin, Carol in Cedar Valley and Gertrude goes to Portland, Oregon, the 5th of this month to take nurse's training at a hospital. Christian and Niels have rented (illegible) farm, a mile away, and 3 hundred acres alongside the farm that they have rented. Carl will run it.

At home we are all well, and the boys are busy husking corn. Dear friends, do write a line. I know, dear Christian, that you do not have much time but when you get started it will not take long to write a letter. I often think if I only could talk to you, but then I remember with joy the little time we had together. Agatha is a big girl by now, and little Ethan can run around and get into things.

My letter did not get done, and today there was a letter from Viggo. We were glad to hear from him. I was afraid he would not write anymore. Loving greetings from us all and first and last from me.

Your aunt,

Johanne Nielsen

Since her last letter Christian has moved from Philadelphia to a parish near Moorhead, Iowa, and Laurine and her family have moved to Tyler, Minnesota, a thriving Danish community with a well-known folk high school called Danebod. This letter contains the first indication of Johanne's illness, and it is also the first in which Pauline, the youngest daughter, is mentioned. Agriculture is flourishing after the economic slump of the 1880s and early 1890s. The mention of the book near the end of the letter reflects the practice of reading sermons at home by devout Christians cut off from a church of their denomination or ethnic group.

Algona, Iowa
September 30, 1901

Dear friends (Christian and Dora),

It is now time I write to you. We have now received two letters from you and the book you sent, for which I thank you many times. When I heard you were coming to Iowa, I thought I would wait with the money till you came, hoping you would come this way and visit us. Or maybe I could come where you are, but I see that it is far from here. If it only had been near Minnesota.

I do not know if you have heard that C. Andersen has moved here from Washington with his family. They live in Tyler, Minnesota. Maybe I will get up there this winter. The doctor says a little trip would do me good.

I have been seeing the doctor for 3 months, but it has not helped the least bit. I have not been well for the past year. It is a strange illness. I have no appetite for any food, and I cannot swallow anything except a little liquid. There is nothing wrong with my throat. The doctors say it is nerve trouble. I work every day because I am not really sick, but I get so tired I almost collapse. There is so much to do, and Pauline and I are alone with it.

Ella went to Washington with Sine (Carol). The boys have bought a mower. We have two hired men besides our own boys. The one we got when the girls left. We will keep him till the corn is husked . The other we got from Prosset. We have had a very good crop this year, one hundred fifty tons of hay. They are all well. Herman has not been this well since we came to America.

We had a letter from Niels in Copenhagen a while ago. I was so glad to hear from him. He sent many little pictures he had taken. He wrote they are all well in Fredericia. He sent a small picture of your father's house. He had taken it himself. It is a long time since I have heard from Denmark.

Please, dear Christian, greet Viggo many times from us when you write to him. I owe him a letter, but it is hard for me to write. I send herewith a money order for $2.50 and thank you many times for the book. It is the best sermon book I have seen.

I really would love to see you again, but it is too far west. I had hoped when I heard that you were coming to Iowa that you should have come nearer to us.

When you write, let me know how much it costs from you to us. I am sending you a picture of me. The one you have does not look like me. Many loving greetings from us all, but first and last from me.

Your aunt,

Johanne Nielsen

This is the picture of Christian and Dorthea's children, Agathe and Ethan, that is mentioned in their grandfather's Christmas letter.

A photograph of Agatha and Ethan leads their grandfather to express spiritual concerns for their lives. It is obvious from Anders' words that Christian comes from a family that is deeply religious and that places the highest emphasis upon the individual's relationship to God in every aspect of life. He then discusses various family members. This letter first mentions that Johanne has been hospitalized in Algona, and it also indicates that Viggo is on his way to Denmark to visit his parents.

Fredericia, Denmark
May 19, 1902

Dear son and daughter-in-law (Christian and Dora),

We wish you the comfort of God's mercy, love and peace from our Lord and Savior, Jesus Christ.

We have the photographs of your little children. Thank you so very much. They are two delightful children. They stand there so happy and open, as children do who are not conscious of any sin. Looking at them, I cannot help praying, "Lord, do not take them out of the world but preserve them in the world." That is surely what you also pray the Father for your dear little ones. You would hate to lose them - it would cut you to the heart if the Lord took them from you. But there is one thing that hurts worse - when children grow up estranged from a godly life. How many parents must say, if only the Lord had taken the children when they were small, we would have been spared this sorrow of seeing them wandering in the way of sin. I would wish and pray God that you will not have to bear such a sorrow in your life.

We long to hear how you are doing in your new home and if you are well. We have been sick this winter. I got well quickly but your mother has been very sick the whole winter since February and still is not well. Now she is only lacking the strength in her legs to walk. She cannot walk alone. We hope though it will be better when it warms up. We have not had any warm weather yet this summer.

We had a letter from Tante Johanne. She is not well. As far as we can tell from the letter she is not at home but in an Algona hospital.

We had a letter from Niels for Pentecost. They are all well. We have also had a letter from Otto. They are well, but work is slack. They have only worked 6 hours a day all winter, but now they work 8 hours. Weimars are well except for Henrik. He was apprenticed to a furniture maker but got sick almost right away. Lately he thought to go back, but lasted only a couple of days.

When he does not do anything he is pretty well, but if he works it is the same again. It is the heart.

We are expecting Viggo in 8 days if all goes well. It would be nice if we could see you every once in a while. Warmest greetings from Weimars, Caroline and your parents and parents-in-law.

A. Christiansen

A note of tenderness pervades this final letter that Johanne writes to Christian. After describing her illness including her extended stay at Rochester and the arrangements made to have her live in Algona for the winter so that she would be near the doctors, she reports that Julia has been married. She closes by entreating Christian to pray for her and write to her. Although she does not expect to see them again, she cannot help wishing that she might.

Algona, Iowa
July 21, 1902

Dear Christian and family,

Thank you many times for your welcome letter. I have waited to hear from you and have often thought to write to you but have not done so. I am so sorry Dora is not well and I hope she will soon be well. I can see from your letter you do not have much time to write.

Unfortunately, I have plenty of time. I will let you know how things are with me. I have been sick for two years and there seems to be no help for me. I was in the hospital in Rochester, Minnesota, for 3 months last winter. They tried to cure me with instruments. I was a little better but then got sick again and was in bed for 3 weeks. The doctor came 3 times a day to see me. Then I went to a hotel near by but then they sent me home. They could see it would be too long before they could do anything for me as long as I was sick.

They wrote to the doctor here in town about what ails me and what instruments he should use when I got well. He had to buy them just for me. Over 50 doctors saw me and none could say what is wrong with me. I was so sick a month after I came home that we rented a room in town, that was the last of March, and now I have been here since and go to the doctor every day. I cannot stand living like this so I will go back to Minnesota again and see whether they can do something for me. With great difficulty I can swallow just enough so I can stay alive and that is all. Gertrude and I will go to Rochester the last of this week or the first of next, God willing. I had to send for her when I was down there during the winter. She has been home since then.

They are all well on the farm. You do not know that Julia was married two months ago to Charles' brother, Jens Andersen. They live in Seattle, Washington.

I am so glad to see you have so many meetings and church services. I have often wondered why I always have to live so far from other children of God, but I think the good God, in His love and wisdom, has laid illness and loneliness on me to draw me closer to Him. Pray for me, dear friends, that I may be firm in faith, patient in troubles and constant in prayer. If you had been here, dear Christian, I would have much to talk to you about, but I suppose I will never see any of you again. But if it is God's will that I get well, I hope to visit you. Nothing is dearer to me than to be with some of God's children. No one who has not tried it can understand the loneliness.

If, dear Christian, you can find a little time to write me, I will be very happy. Just use the old address, they will send it to me. Now I will close with many loving greetings from them all at home, and first and last from me.

Your aunt,

Johanne Nielsen

HAN 988 6-2-39 Danish

The terminal nature of Johanne's illness is revealed in this letter from the recently married Julia. There is also a request for the recipe of a medicine that had been described in the Danish-American publication, Hyrderøsten.

Algona, Iowa
October 3, 1902

Rev. C. C. Mengers
Moorhead, Iowa

Dear cousin Christian,

You no doubt will be surprised at receiving a letter from your cousin Julia. I came home from the West two weeks ago today. Ella also came with me. She is going to stay at home all winter. I do not know how long I will stay, but I think I will go back about the tenth of this month.

Mamma was very sick when we first came home, but she is getting a little better. Of course you know that mamma's case is incurable. They will have nothing more to do with her at the hospital. They say they have done all they can for her. But there is no telling how long she may live. The doctors say it may be for months.

Mamma does not know all of this so, when you write her, please do not let her know her condition because it worries her dreadfully. Mamma asked me to ask you to tell them in Denmark that she is still alive and will write to you and them as soon as she is able.

Will you please send mamma a receipt you have in a Danish paper Hurde Rysten. (Don't laugh at my spelling for I haven't the least idea how that should be spelled.) One ingredient she says is hemp seed. She thinks if she only could get that it would make her stronger.

Give my best regards to your wife and yourself.

Your sincere cousin,

Julia Andersen

Algona Iowa,
Nov. 2, 1902.

Dear Cousin Christian,

Our beloved mother passed away Monday after noon at 4 oclock, October 27. She did not speak to us. She was sleeping it seemed peacefully and never moved at all. I went to her and placed my finger on her pulse and it had stoped, but it must not have been very many minutes before.

She always spoke so much of your father and mother. She waited

In an earlier day, recipients were alerted that a letter was notifying them of death by the black edges of the envelope and stationery. This is the letter that informed Christian of Tante Johanne's death.

96

This is the inevitable letter edged in black that prepared the recipient for a message of death. In it Gertrude describes her mother's death. She expresses her sorrow and sense of loss in poignant words.

Algona, Iowa
November 2, 1902

Dear cousin Christian,

Our beloved mother passed away Monday afternoon at 4 o'clock, October 27. She did not speak to us. She was sleeping it seemed peacefully and never moved at all. I went to her and placed my finger on her pulse and it had stopped, but it must not have been very many minutes before.

She always spoke so much of your father and mother. She waited so long to find out whether Viggo had returned or not. She wished to know all about the people in Denmark. Will you please write to your mother? I wish that I could write Danish so that I could write to them all. Papa is such a poor hand at writing letters.

Mamma had been sick so long and suffered so much that we knew of course that she would not be with us much longer, but she was so patient and hopeful until the last that I could not believe that she was going to die. Some times it seems to me if I could but have her back just one week I could let her go.

She received your letter just a few days before she died. She spoke so often of your little girl. I have never wished before as I do now that I had known all of my aunties and uncles that I might have written to them.

When you write to Viggo will you tell him that I should like very much to hear from him?

And now I expect you to let your people know of our sad loss, and hope to hear from you soon.

Your affectionate cousin,

Gertrude Nielsen

Some perceptive comments on Christmas open this letter from Christian's father, Anders Christiansen, who makes use of the beautiful old Danish saying that Christmas lasts till Easter. He then comments on Johanne's death, her spiritual restlessness in life, and his sincere hope that now "all her needs are filled."

Fredericia, Denmark
December 18, 1902

Dear son and daughter-in-law (Christian and Dora),

The great Christmas holiday is approaching and we wish that it may be a blessed Christmas for you and for ourselves. Christmas is the children's festival, and may we who are old become as children so we can in childlike faith receive the news of Jesus our Savior's birth. Then we can have a happy Christmas. Everyone who can be glad is so at Christmas, but if Jesus is not in our Christmas joy it is a poor joy. While many are happy at Christmas, there are those who are not, perhaps because they lack the necessities of life, or health to enjoy life's good things. And so they cannot hear the angels' song from Bethlehem. When you get this letter your Christmas will be over, but we will still wish you a happy Christmas because the old saying is that Christmas lasts till Easter. And we will wish you a happy new year remaining well to live with your dear little children.

We have not been well lately. Caroline and Mother were in bed at the same time. They are not able to get out yet, but at least they are out of bed. We must be satisfied with that. We are waiting to hear if Dora is well after her operation and if you are all well.

Tante Johanne has died according to a message from Viggo. Herman has not written about it, though he should have. We have the hope that she died saved. We enjoyed her when she was here visiting us. She was so sad that she had to live in so spiritually dead a place, where there was nothing good to hear and very little fellowship with other of God's children. Now we hope all her needs are filled, and that God will help us all to meet with her in the Father's house. God help us all and give us grace to fight against anything that would distract us from grace in Christ Jesus.

Loving greetings from Weimars, Caroline and your parents and in-laws.

A. Christiansen

HAN 988 6-3-7 Danish

There is a slight note of reprimand in this letter from Gertrude, and one wonders what parish demands prevented Christian from writing to the family following Johanne's death. Dorthea, however, had undergone surgery in the intervening months. The letter reveals that Viggo who was recently married and his wife Dora had made a trip to Denmark and that their aunt Ane Kristine had moved back to Illinois from Alabama. It also contains a few short sentences about Johanne's last days.

Algona, Iowa
January 29, 1903

Dear cousin Christian,

I wrote you telling you of our dear mother's death in October, but have not heard whether you ever received it or not, so I thought that I would drop you a few words now.

I have wanted to know for ever so long whether Viggo ever returned to Philadelphia. He wrote me a few days before he sailed, and said that he expected to return in August. He has never written since. I suppose he does not know that mamma is dead.

She received your letter a few days before she died. She was so near gone, when it came, that I do not think she ever finished reading it. She spoke of you only a day or two before she died.

I suppose that you know Aunt Ankristeen (Ane Kristine) has left Alabama and is again in Streator, Ill. She could not make a living in that place any longer. I think that she is living with Mary(Mae) at present.

You wrote once that your wife expected to go to a hospital and have an operation. Did she go? If she did, I sincerely hope that it was successful and beneficial. And now won't you please write and send me Viggo's address, and tell us how you are getting along?

I remain as ever,

Your affectionate cousin,

Gertrude K. Nielsen

Top: A picture of one of the Algona railroad stations that captures the aura of Carol's description. (Courtesy of the Kossuth County Historical Society)

Bottom: Tante Johanne's weathered gravestone bearing the simple inscription, "MOTHER," remains today very much as Carol describes it in her letter.

This descriptive letter, which breaks a six-year lapse, contains the account of Carol and Gertrude's return to Algona to visit the grave of Johanne. Carol obviously had not been back for the funeral, and the letter not only describes the grave but offers some interesting observations on Algona. On their return trip to Washington and on Gertrude's subsequent journey to Alaska they narrowly escaped several serious accidents. Accounts of these events appeared in the New York <u>Tribune</u> and the Denver <u>Post</u>.

Black Diamond
King County, Washington
September 19, 1909

My dear cousin Christian,

Gertie (Gertrude) and I arrived here August 23rd and she took a boat from Seattle for Alaska Aug. 25th. There was a great time getting her off but she, poor tired girl, got off. We had a hard trip home this time, the hardest we have ever had. The trains were so crowded that we could not get any sleepers, and Gertie had to get home, so there was no choice, we had to stop off at night and ride in the day coach in the daytime.

We went up to Algona. It lies there the same sleepy little town as ever. The first thing I noticed was that the same old iron stove and old wooden seats were in that Northwestern depot as when I came to Algona as a child. They have not even received a new coat of paint. We went right from the depot to the graveyard, and I can't tell you how much better I feel to know where all that is left in this world of my mother lies. She is in a beautiful spot, and there was just one beautiful white flower on her grave. The boys selected a pretty little stone with the word "Mother" on it.

From there we went to see some of our friends. Everybody that we have ever known came to see us. We only stayed a few days and then started west. We had to lay over three nights to get from southern Iowa to Algona. At Denver there were two trains going west, one at 8:00 a.m. and one at 9:00 a.m. Gertie was determined to go at 8:00 a.m. as she wanted to reach Seattle as quickly as possible. I would not go because I wanted to wait till the post office opened so as to hear from Neal. I was afraid we wouldn't hear at Salt Lake. After a great to-do, I succeeded in getting her to wait just one hour. Well, we got our letter and started at 9. We had scarcely gone 10 miles when our train stopped for all day. The train we missed by that letter was wrecked and 59 people injured and 12 killed. Our train pulled up, and we saw the dreadful sight, 3 coaches in the ditch and three engines too. Well, our train killed a man, and we came over the mountains with the wheel loose on our car.

We had been in so much trouble that we were glad to see dear old Seattle. Gertie was going to go to Alaska on the "Ohio," but it left Seattle the day before she arrived and so she took another boat, Well, the "Ohio" sank with a loss of about 12 lives. It seems as if she was to escape both times. I have only had one card from her. She said that they passed the "Ohio," and all they could see of her was her smoke stack.

We found everybody well. I have been very busy. My school opened the week I returned, and I have bought furniture and set up a little housekeeping establishment. I like it very much. I hope this finds you all well. Give my very best regards to Dora and the children. Tell Viggo that I'm going to write him within a few days.

Your loving cousin,

Carol Nielsen

P.S. Father is getting better every day.

After reporting that her father and Ane Kristine (Herman had married Johanne's sister in the intervening years and had moved to Alabama) have returned to Chicago, Gertrude presents a vivid description of life in Alaska among the native Americans where for six months of the year she is the only white woman. Whether she is in Shakan only as a teacher or whether she also functions as a nurse, is not clear.

Shakan, Alaska
March 14, 1910

Dear cousin Christian,

I wrote to you when I first came to Shakan, but have had no reply, so suppose that you never received it.

I would have written again before this but had mislaid your address.

I suppose that you know that papa is now living in Chicago. I am glad that they left Alabama. I did not like it down there. One of the women Carol and I met while there, has written me several letters. She said in her last one, that they had had the coldest winter that she had ever experienced down there.

We have had more snow at Shakan this winter than has ever been seen here before. At two different times it fell 24 inches in a night. We saw the sun today at school for the first time since about October 10th. The hills or mountains are so high that it does not rise above them for so many months so you see the snow does not melt unless it rains and we have had only three days of rain since Christmas, so the snow kept falling and piling up until we had at least seven feet on the level. I have not minded it much because it has not been at all cold excepting two or three days when the thermometer fell to 1 degree above zero which is the coldest weather we have had.

It has been rather a unique experience for me, but am not sorry that I have spent the winter here. I have been and will be the only white woman within a distance of 145 miles since Oct. 19 when a large ship came in and took all the white people down to the states. We had expected some back by this time (March 1st) but there has been so much snow that the marble quarry and cannery will not open until May 1st and that is when I leave. We have been just three white people here since then, one who is manager of the Company Store and another who comes and goes.

There are quite a few well educated Indians and one little woman who has been very kind to me, looks as white as I. She is a half-breed but is a graduate from a college in the States. I hardly know what I should have done without her.

The natives (Indians) are much more intelligent than the poor whites of the South. The Government is doing splendid work for them and also the Mission Schools.

I really love the little children. They have such a winning way about them.

The Government has asked me to come back next year, but hardly think I shall do so. One thing, our nearest doctor is at Juneau, Alaska about 150 or 200 miles away.

I felt rather lonesome and blue the night last October when the boat steamed away with some people here who had been so very kind to me, and did not dare look ahead or think of the months stretched out before me, but I am surprised to see how nicely I have gotten along. The natives have been very careful to see that I did not lack venison, fish and clams. I have found it very cheap to live here.

Two of the women each gave me a real Indian basket for Christmas. They are getting quite rare as the younger generation do not know how to make them.

I do not think that it will be many years before these natives will be entirely extinct. They are all tubercular and are dying off very rapidly with Consumption. It is because they will not take care of themselves. Today with the snow almost covering our schoolhouse I had some pupils come with their bare feet in their shoes, and it is not at all unusual to see babies 2 and 3 years old running around in the snow barefoot.

I have learned many new things this winter, but I am beginning to feel that I am glad I shall get back to Seattle in about six more weeks. I am going to take a different route out from here than the one I came in. This will give me an opportunity to see very nearly every other town in South East Alaska which I have not visited.

The Totem poles and old graveyards are extremely interesting. It is peculiar to see how much these Indians follow the same customs as do the Chinese and Japanese.

We visited the Shakan cemetery one day and a short time before this a baby had died. Its parents belonged to The Salvation Army and though they had a long sermon there and tolled the bell, still we found fresh fruit, oranges, apples etc. placed in a dish on the grave and also all the child's belongings, a chair, a little drum etc.

Another thing, these Indians do not resemble the Eastern Tribes at all. If they were living in the States many would be passed off as white and the others as Orientals - Japs or Chinese. They do not have the high cheek bones. Neither are they indolent, but are quite progressive. Almost every family owns a gasoline launch and some of these are worth as much as $3,000. We have three boat-building establishments worked entirely by Indians.

It is wonderful to see what the Presbyterian Church has accomplished in this town. All the natives belong to either The Salvation Army or The Presbyterian Church and they are very strict in their dealings. I have perfect faith in their honesty. It is considered a disgrace for one of them to smoke, drink or do anything like that. I have not seen tobacco used excepting by one of the white men here. They are very musical and several play the organ and piano, while they have a splendid band.

I wish you could see our scenery. It is magnificent. The mountains covered very nearly to the top with evergreens and capped with snow on which the sunshine casts the most brilliant hues.

I would rather now live in Alaska than in Iowa or the East.

I expect to return next year but shall endeavor to be placed somewhere on the Yukon River or near Fairbanks.

I am afraid you are tiring of this so shall just ask how everyone is? I hope you are looking stronger than you did last summer and that those dear children of yours are strong as ever. I want you to give my love to Dora, your wife. I think she is such a lovely woman. If you can find time to drop me a line before I leave here I shall appreciate it very much.

Do go and see father when you can.

Sincerely,

Gertrude K. Nielsen

Viggo and Dora's marriage was not the happiest, resulting in periods of separation. During one of these Christian heard that Viggo was lonely and ill in Washington. He asked Carol to attempt to locate Viggo. This is her response containing news about Gertrude and Ella as well as Viggo.

South Bend, Washington
July 14, 1910

My dear cousin Christian,

I came down here to look up Viggo. I stopped off at Menlo and then came on to South Bend. At Menlo they told me that he had been there a week ago and that he was perfectly well. I find that he has lots of friends and is getting along nicely.

They tell me here that he has gone out to the seashore, which is about 12 miles from here. It is fine out there and just as cheap to stay there so I don't wonder he went.

The report that you got is wrong. I don't see how such falsehoods get out to worry about. You need not worry any more about him. By what people tell me, he has had work just about all of the time he has been here.

He has written me some very cheerful letters, and he has just been a little lazy about writing to you.

Just you take my advice and don't let him worry you any more. I wish I could have seen him, but people speak as if he was perfectly happy here. And none of them have heard that he has been sick at all. So don't worry anymore. I am sure he will get a good position next year. They speak very highly of him as a teacher here.

The rest of us are all well. Gertie and Ella are going way up to Fort Yukon this year. I will write you again. I am in a hurry to send this before I leave here. I have lost your address so I will send this to Pauline.

Write to me at Black Diamond, Wash. and send me your address. Give my love to Dora and the children.

Your affectionate cousin,

Carol Nielsen

HAN 988 4-1-48 English

Thirty-three years elapse between the last letter and this. That there was some correspondence is evident from the opening paragraph of this letter, but thus far nothing has been discovered in the archives for the intervening years. As with so many other immigrants, this Danish family undoubtedly gave to the United States as much as it received. Johanne's nephew, Christian, was made a Knight of the Order of Dannebrog by King Frederik IX of Denmark for promoting Danish-American relations. Another nephew, Viggo, translated Scandinavian, French and German communications during World War II for the United States government. Johanne's grandson, H. Carl Andersen, Laurine's son, was a twelve term congressman from Minnesota. Contributions by other of Johanne's descendant as preserved at this time in the Danish Immigrant Archive - Dana College may not have been as spectacular, but they were the solid efforts of teachers, nurses, farmers, businessmen, homemakers, and during World War II, service personnel.

This letter, though it falls far beyond the 1887-1910 years used in the title of the book, provides a fitting conclusion for a work on Tante Johanne and her family. Although Johanne never became Americanized but always longed for Denmark and the old ways, her family was quite different. They were completely American and as this letter indicates her grandchildren served in various branches of the military during World War II. During the years following Johanne's death, Carol has married and several of Johanne's children have died. Now Carol, whose childhood letter opened this collection, is seventy-one. She had immigrated to America as a child and once considered revisiting Denmark, the land of her birth. Now Hitler and the War have changed all that. Instead she is content to remain in Washington, a state that she truly loves. As she reflects on life and her departed loved ones, she observes, " Life is so short, but sometimes I think they are spared a lot. The world is so hard now."

3002 W 62 ST.
Seattle, Washington
February 27, 1943

Dear cousin Christian,

I intended to write to you long before this, and in looking over my files, I find that a year has slipped by, since I heard from you. In that letter you said that you wished you had that picture where we were all seven sisters in a row. So I took mine to a photographer and had it copied and I am sending it to you. I hope you will like it. I tried to get it for Christmas, but you know we have to wait for everything now.

Sister Gertrude's son is in the army and we have not heard from him for a long time. We are afraid he has gone overseas. Sister May's (Marie, Mae) granddaughter joined the WAVEs and is now in New York in training. Sister Ella has a son in the Pacific somewhere. He wrote to us, but he could not tell us where he is, and Ella's other son will be in the next draft.

Often I think of our cousins in Denmark. I wonder how they are getting along. I know we have many relatives there, but the only ones I have seen are two cousins on our father's side. They came over here years ago and lived here in Seattle for about a year and then went back to Denmark. They were at my wedding. The oldest one's name is Lorena. I hope Hitler has not harmed them or our other cousins. I mean your brother and sister Caroline. You know my mother was over in Denmark before she died and she often told me what a dear girl Caroline was. I would have liked to have met her. Do you hear from her, and are they suffering under Hitler's government. I so often think of them. If the war had not come, I might have taken a trip to Europe. I was thinking seriously of it but I did not get off before the war and now I do not want to go. I hope and pray that this cruel war will soon be over. I took a trip east last summer. I went to California to visit Ella. She lives in Fresno. She has a nice family of three boys and one girl, all nice, bright children. And from there I went to Spencer, Iowa and visited my brothers Niel (Niels) and Chris (Christian). You know our brother Carl died. I don't know if you knew that Julia and Pauline (the youngest one) and May all have gone home I hope. I miss them so, especially Julia. Life is so short, but sometimes I think they are spared a lot. The world is so hard now.

Brother Chris has not been very well for quite a while. He did not look well to me but brother Niel looked fine. From Iowa I went to Tyler, Minn. to visit sister Lorena (Laurine). Her husband has been sick for about four or five years, he has heart trouble and he is totally blind. They have to stay right by him night and day. Sister Rena (Laurine) sits by him in the day time and her daughter Julia at night. I am so sorry for all of them. Poor Carl is just as patient as he can be but still it is hard. They all took me for rides so as to see the country. It is a nice country but so different from Wash. I am afraid I could not love that country as much as Washington.

I am sorry I could not have seen you and Dora but I only had a round trip ticket so I had to come home. We have had a very cold winter this year. We had some snow, something we do not often see.

Love and best wishes to you and Dora.

Your loving cousin,

Carol N. George

This is the picture of Tante Johanne's seven daughters taken many years earlier which Carol sends to Christian in 1943. They are arranged by age, youngest to eldest, from left to right: Pauline, Ella, Gertrude, Julia, Carol, Marie (Mae) and Laurine.

Works Cited

Fuller, Wayne E. The Old Country School. Chicago: University of Chicago Press, 1982.

Garland, Hamlin. A Son of the Middle Border. Lincoln, Nebraska: Bison Press, 1979.

Glad, Paul W. McKinley, Bryan, and the People. New York: J.B. Lippincott Co., 1964.

Hicks, John D. The Populist Revolt. Lincoln, Nebraska: University of Nebraska, 1961.

History of Kossuth County 1912-1976. Lake Mills, Iowa: Graphic Publishing Co., Inc., 1976.

Lutz, Charles P., ed. Church Roots. Minneapolis: Augsburg Publishing House, 1985.

Marzolf, Marion T. The Danish-Language Press in America. New York: Arno Press, 1979.

Merk, Frederick. History of the Westward Movement. New York: Alfred A. Knopf, 1978.

Miller, Karen. Karen Miller's Diary. Northfield, Minnesota: Unpublished, but mimeographed bound copy, n.d.

Swett, John. American Public Schools. New York: American Book Co., 1900.

Winther, Sophus Keith. Take All to Nebraska, Lincoln. Nebraska: Bison Press, 1976.

R. 30 W. R. 29 W. R. 28 W. R. 27 W.

EAGLE

GRANT

SPRINGFIELD

HEBRON

T. 100 N.

SWEA

HARRISON

LEDYARD

LINCOLN

T. 99 N.

SENECA

GREENWOOD

RAMSEY

GERMAN

T. 98 N.

FENTON

BURT

PORTLAND

BUFFALO

T. 97 N.

LOTTS CREEK

UNION

PLUM CREEK

WESLEY

T. 96 N.

WHITTEMORE

CRESCO

IRVINGTON

PRAIRIE

T. 95 N.

GARFIELD

RIVERDALE

SHERMAN

LUVERNE

T. 94 N.

111

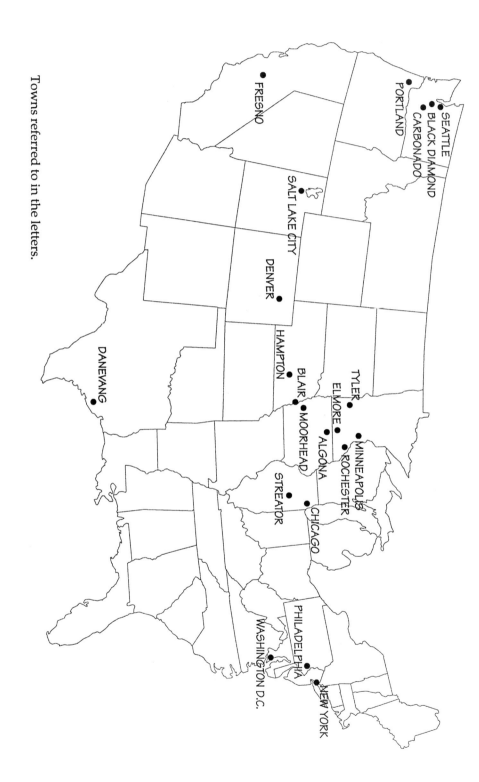

Towns referred to in the letters.

SEATTLE
BLACK DIAMOND
CARBONADO
PORTLAND
FRESNO
SALT LAKE CITY
DENVER
DANEVANG
HAMPTON
BLAIR
MOORHEAD
TYLER
ELMORE
ALGONA
MINNEAPOLIS
ROCHESTER
STREATOR
CHICAGO
PHILADELPHIA
WASHINGTON D.C.
NEW YORK

112

Nielsen - Christiansen Family

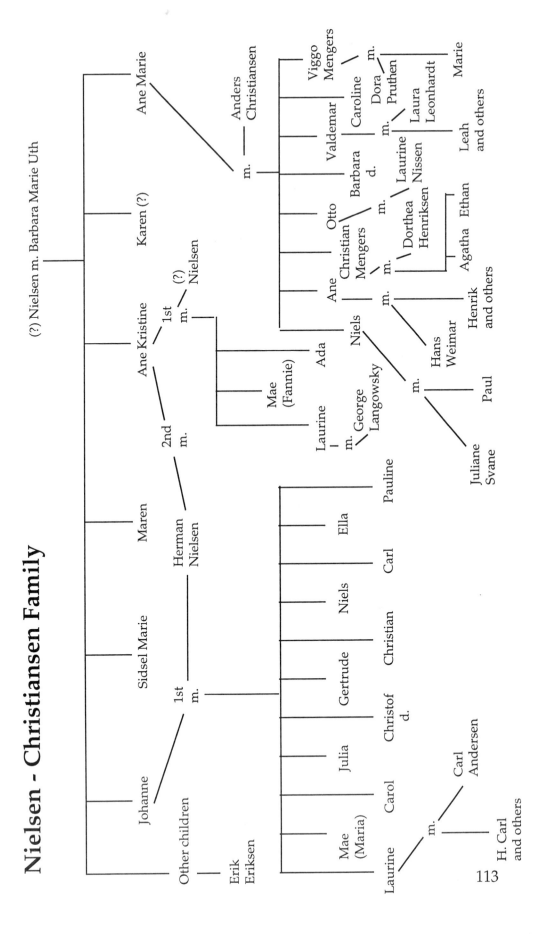

(?) Nielsen m. Barbara Marie Uth

113

Index

Page numbers indicate the beginning of the letter in which the reference is found

116

Lur Publications
Policies and Personnel

Lur Publications is designed to encourage research and scholarship on Danish immigrant subjects as well as making available to the general public materials in the Danish Immigrant Archive - Dana College. As such Lur Pulications complements the goals of the Danish American Heritage Society.

A further aim is to promote the collection, preservation, cataloging and use of written materials produced and received by Danish immigrants and their descendants. Such materials are welcomed by the respective Danish Immigrant Archives located at Dana and Grand View Colleges. Artifacts associated with Danish immigrants are sought by the Danish Immigrant Museum in Elk Horn, Iowa.

Scholars wishing to submit manuscripts for consideration are invited to contact Lur Publications, Danish Immigrant Archive, Dana College, Blair, Nebraska 68008-1041,(402) 426-7300, FAX: (402) 426-7332, e-mail: library@acad2.dana.edu

 # Lur Publications Personnel

Editor-in-chief: Dr. John W. Nielsen
Advisory Board: Dr. Myrvin Christopherson, Dr. Paul Formo, Dr. John Mark Nielsen, Ruth Rasmussen
Library Staff: Ruth Rasmussen, Sharon Jensen, Mary Bacon, JoAnn Hohensee, Thomas Nielsen
Student Assistants: Kevin Harrison, Jennifer Doerfler, Ann Gibbs, Sherry Guyett, Marnie Jensen, Sarah Peterson
Archive Volunteers to 1996: Marian Anderson, Norman Bansen, Elaine Christensen, Ninna Engskow, Charles Hansen,Edward Hansen, Ethan Hansen, Florence M. Hansen, Gerald Hansen, Janice Hansen, Pat Hansen, Sara Hansen-Walter, Shirley Hansen, Helga Hanson, Verlan Hanson, Jill Hennick, Carol Johnson, Dolores (Dody) Johnson, Bernice (Bee) Krantz, Inga Larsen, Lorraine Madsen, Margaret Madsen, Eunice Neve, Paul Neve, David Nielsen, Elizabeth Nielsen, John W. Nielsen, Luella Nielsen, Ruth Herman Nielsen, Richard Schuler, Marion Svendsen, Dorothy Wright, Harold Wright.